THE TRIAL OF MY LIFE

THE TRIAL OF MY LIFE

JOSEPH D. VALENTINO
WITH SHEILA KENNEDY

To my wife, Janet, you have been steady and true ...
for all these years ...

TABLE OF CONTENTS

ACKNOWLEDGMENTS

MY SONS:

You, and the entire family, have always been "first" in any life decision made by me.

Your love and understanding made it less difficult to leave the daily Hall of Justice controversies and sadness behind when I came home at night.

Without my family, there would not have been a Judge Joseph D. Valentino.

MY SECRETARY, KIM:

You endured a legal life of "ups and downs"... sometimes humorous ... but most times serious and stressful. Many of your memories are in these pages.

Always loyal and faithful ... polite and caring to others ... you were undoubtedly the very best professional assistant ... and always, a trusted friend.

ALL LAW ASSISTANTS ... APPOINTED AND ASSIGNED:

To Valerie, Dan, Bill, Miguel, Diane, Steve, and Anne among many others:

Your hard work and knowledge of the law made me a much better judge. I will always remember our discussions, both law and life related which influenced much of this book. I also sincerely appreciate how you often worked tirelessly to make my public speeches knowledgeable and coherent!

ALL THE JUDGES, ATTORNEYS AND COURT STAFF

I see your faces and hear your voices. Thank you for your support and advice as well as your legal arguments and your opinions. All of which have shaped my legal life and are quite often found in this book.

ALL COURT ATTENDANTS AND DEPUTY SHERIFFS ... ESPECIALLY JOHN AND ANGELO

I realize that your job was to protect me. You did it with professionalism and dignity and through the years you became cherished friends. You will remember all of these stories ... you have lived through them.

SHEILA KENNEDY ... MY CO-AUTHOR

I want to sincerely thank my co-author and publisher. She interviewed me for countless hours and suffered through hearing the same stories more than once! She was always "up" and confident. I will always be grateful to her.

FOREWORD

BY SHEILA KENNEDY

Judge Valentino has been a part of my life since the day I was born. He and my dad were lifelong friends since their time at Aquinas together, and I have fond memories of "Uncle Joe" from when I was little. As I got older, I remember walking in a parade when he was running for City Court with a T-shirt on that said *Please Vote for My Uncle Joe*. I honestly never in a million years would have thought I would help him write his memoir.

I remember reading the article in the paper about him when he retired, thinking that he should write a book. I wasn't a publisher yet, and had no idea what was in store, until I met the Judge again at my brother's wedding reception in May 2016. We "reunited" that day after not seeing each other for 20+ years. We talked that day about writing books, and he said he had heard I might be someone that could help him with that. I gave him my card and honestly didn't expect it to go anywhere.

He called me about five days later and said let's talk. It was my first indication to the depth of this man that I have grown to absolutely adore. He said he was going to call me, and he did. That means so much in a world that has more people acting without integrity than with it. As we started the interviews for the book content, I knew that I had stumbled onto a treasure in this man.

The Judge is fair, just, respectful and thoughtful. He is a man of character—the kind of man I tell my daughter to hold out for. He is fun and social too. His talents are not limited to the courtroom. He is musically talented, athletic, compassionate and giving.

It sounds a little like hero worship and that may not be far off the mark. What is fascinating to me is that everyone who knows the Judge feels the same way about him. There was no dirt to uncover or skeletons to bury. Everyone who I have come in contact with says the same thing about the Judge. As the character witness testimonies came in, I read over and over what a good man he is. Some moved me to tears because the statements his friends, colleagues and family made dripped with truth and were written so sincerely. Everything about Uncle Joe is genuine and from the heart. It was so clearly evident that anyone who knows him agrees.

Judge Valentino is a humble man and is most likely uncomfortable with all of the nice things that people say about him. He has such a sincere desire to be good to other people and to see the good in them. He expects no accolades or fanfare. I believe the greatest tribute anyone could give him is to be a good person, acting with compassion and respect, because they saw that in him.

My life has sincerely been blessed since starting this book with the Judge. I believe after reading his story, that yours will be too. Unfortunately, it is rare to find great examples for good living in this world. This story of the Judge's life, both on and off the bench, will present you with hope that the world is still a good place, and there are honorable people still in it.

We set up this book loosely as a trial, complete with Sidebar material, character witnesses, opening and closing statements and a verdict at the end. Judge Valentino loved trial work and the drama of the courtroom. (I think it might be because he never parented teenage daughters and their "drama"!) Seriously though, I couldn't think of a more fitting way to examine the legacy of honor, respect and compassion he leaves than to put his life on trial by a jury of his peers.

Enjoy!

INTRODUCTION

It's a cold January morning in Rochester, NY. I'm a couple of weeks into my retirement from the bench. I feel a little lost without going into a courtroom after having entered a courtroom almost daily for over 40 years. Every day was an adventure regardless of my role. Not everyone can say that they had a career that fulfilled them. I am one of those for-

Reading the newspaper article about my retirement in the Democrat and Chronicle.

tunate enough to say not only did my legal career fulfill me, but I was gratefully given several opportunities to make contributions to justice.

Today there is an article in the *Democrat and Chronicle* about me. Gary Craig has been writing about the happenings in my courtrooms since 1998. It is fitting that he wrote the article about my retirement. I'm proud and humbled by the headline, *"Retiring Judge Brought Humanity to the Bench—For 33 years Joseph Valentino has sought compassion in his rulings."*

No matter what role I have assumed in my life, whether it was as a lawyer or judge, dignity in each human life, and holding respect for that humanity, has always been important to me. I'm humbled that people may remember me for that.

It is interesting that the article shares my experience with the Bird Lady. She was quite a character. When I think about it, it is actually an appropriate case to highlight, because I sentenced her in a way that was alternative to jail. I knew jail was not going to be a good fit for her. That sentence—for her to stay on her medication with periodic check ins—was a foreshadowing of my time in the DTC (Drug Treatment Court). Not everyone who is convicted of a non-violent crime belongs in jail and the famous bird lady was such an example of alternative sentencing.

 SIDEBAR

One day the bailiff came back to tell me that a lady to be arraigned in court on a minor charge, brought a bag with her to use for bail. I asked what was in the bag, and the bailiff replied, "dead squirrels." I told him she would not be needing those today.

When she came up for arraignment, I read the charges, made sure she had a lawyer, and ordered her to see the court psychologist before she comes in again.

The next time she came to court, she was charged with another crime ... cruelty to animals. She was accused of taking feathers from birds and affixing them to statues and figurines in her home. The animal control office claimed that they were responding to reports from neighbors hearing calls of birds in distress. In court, the bird lady came barreling down the aisle wearing a bridal gown. The psychologist reported that she understood the court proceedings, her responsibilities and consequences. The public defender and the ADA said the defendant wouldn't plead guilty, so the case went to trial.

At the first day of the trial, as I entered the courtroom, I saw a duck decoy on the defense table. The defense attorney had an impish grin. I asked him what it was, and he said that she wanted to enter it into evidence.

The bird lady took the stand. She explained that the birds were all dead when she removed the feathers. The animal control officer testified that they had been receiving calls about birds being in distress at the defendant's home. He then attempted to show bird distress calls with his voice. The bird lady objected. She corrected the animal control officer by making her own distress calls. The court reporter looked up to me for guidance on transcript accuracy!

I found her guilty and put her on probation. Conditions of her probation were to attend a clinic, take her medication, and stay away from birds.

Beyond all else, I always wanted to be fair. I am sincerely hopeful I achieved that throughout my career.

Those of you who know the stories, will probably notice that we omitted many specific names. If you were omitted at all, please note that we felt your privacy is important and we, in no way, wanted you or your family to feel uncomfortable or embarrassed. However, I have no problem (and think it would be great) if you read a story and yell out:

"Hey...that's me he's talking about!"

OK ... enough of the introduction. I am hopeful that this "trial" will be interesting for you to read and deliberate before you reach a verdict. It truly is *The Trial of My Life*.

CHAPTER I

PRE-TRIAL DISCOVERY

I was born the only son to my Italian parents, Nick and Anna Valentino, on November 1, 1946. My mom was born in America and the family legend is that my grandmother made sure she delivered my Mom on American soil. My Dad, born in Italy, was named Nicola after his grandfather and my grandfather was named Giuseppe after his grandfather. Hence, I am Joseph and I have a son named Nick. My Mother's Father was named Amodeo Carlini. An immigration officer on

My Mom and Dad, Anna and Nick Valentino

Ellis Island decided that his American name should be Daniel Carlineo; therefore, my middle name is Daniel as I was named after both grandfathers.

Strong Italian traditions were passed onto me by my parents and also my extended family that lived in the neighborhood. Italian was spoken in our house, but never to me. I picked up a little bit, but couldn't carry on a conversation today. Years later when I asked them why they didn't teach me Italian, they said they wanted me to be a true American. Both were very proud to be American citizens and they wanted their son to be accepted and successful. It was their American dream.

To achieve this dream, my Dad, a barber by trade, worked long hours in the shop and my Mom later worked long hours at DuPont while I was in High School and College. I know that they both sacrificed for me to have a good education. There was no question in their minds that I would be the first Valentino to graduate from college.

One reason that they did so much for me is that I was an only child. My mom had a very difficult time in delivery and she was told that she couldn't have any more children after me. I can honestly say that I wasn't spoiled though—they tempered their actions by being strict disciplinarians.

We moved to Montcalm Drive in the suburb of Irondequoit when I was almost twelve years old. Prior to that we lived in the city. It was a small house in Irondequoit and the first thing this "city boy" did after we pulled in the driveway, was to climb the huge tree in the very big backyard. My own backyard equated to happiness. My parents were so happy to have their own house.

As I entered my teen years, my dad passed on the things that fathers teach their sons who are going to make something of themselves. He taught me about respect and pride. My dad taught me how to be ethical and honest. He told me to dress well and look presentable. Always treat others with respect. He reminded me to mind my manners and how to know right from wrong. My parents were not overly religious, but they made certain that I received a Catholic education. They were successful in that objective as I attended a Catholic grammar school, high school, college and law school.

We lived a simple life, and I didn't grow up in a fancy house. I was expected to do as I was told and not to talk back or be disrespectful. As a young man, I was a little rebellious occasionally and any time I attempted to be disrespectful, I reaped the consequences. It didn't take more than once to learn that lesson. It formed how I parented and presided in the years to come. Those lessons from my father shaped the man I am.

I had a dog named Queenie when I was young and we were a part of a group of kids that hung around together almost every day. Like most neighborhoods of the time, they were safe, and we kids would roam and explore without fear. At night, I needed to be home when the street lamps went on and there would be no excuses.

Years ago, I was interviewed and gave an account of my dog to Ross Talarico, who was compiling a collection of stories to highlight the heritage of Italian Americans in Rochester. I thought I would share my own revised and abbreviated version of that interview with you so you could experience an event in my childhood.

My friends and I would often play on the corner hill, or the empty lot next to the "neighborhood widow." She was always dressed in black: the black shawl, the black stockings, the black shoes, no matter what the season, temperature or current fashion. Her house was next to the field where we played baseball and football, and every once in a while, a ball would go over the fence, and she'd be there, as if she was waiting for that moment. That dark solitary figure would appear; she would pick up the ball; stare at us and make her way back to her house. That would always be the end of our game.

One day the football flew over the fence and into her yard. It was too early in the afternoon to do nothing, so in a fit of rebellious courage, I jumped the wooden fence and crouched down making my way through the uncut bushes and weeds. My friends were yelling encouragement. I leaped forward, grabbed the ball, and in a moment of victory I stood up holding the ball and waving it over my head.

It happened very quickly, a shadow over me with a broom whisking through the air. A strange language filling me with terror and suddenly the chase was on. As I ran toward the fence, feeling sure I would be hit on the head with the broom, a blur of golden brown fur jumped the fence and ran past me. As I jumped back over the fence, I looked back and saw Queenie biting the woman's posterior and ripping her black dress as she lay in the jungle of her yard.

That night, I was aware of a "conference" going on in my aunt's kitchen. I feared the worst, and later that evening when my parents told me that Queenie would have to go; I felt for the first time a sense of injustice. The dog was only defending me and coming to my rescue.

The next day when I came home from school, the house was quiet. Her dish was gone. I sadly knew that she, too, was gone.

A great influence in my life was music. There was always music on the radio or from the record player. When I was little, my family couldn't afford a piano or the lessons. My parents did what many families did when they couldn't afford a piano … they bought me an accordion. I did not love the accordion, and I wanted to play a different instrument. I was a bit mischievous and stuck a pencil in it once so it wouldn't work properly.

―――――――――――― **SIDEBAR** ――――――――――――

While in high school, I watched the Beatles on Ed Sullivan, just like thousands of other American teenagers. I decided then that I wanted to play the guitar. I went to a music store carrying my old accordion with me ... Hoping to trade it in for an acoustic guitar. When I inquired about trading it in, the music store owner laughed. He then took me to a room full of old, traded-in accordions. Apparently, I wasn't the only kid in Rochester who didn't like playing the accordion.

―――――――――――――――――――――――――――

Even though no trade was possible, I did come home with a guitar that day (I had saved some money … just in case) and loved it. I played until my fingers bled. I have been a guitarist (or bass player) in many bands over the years, and music influenced how I made money in college and where I went to law school. Later when I took the bench, I still wanted to play but felt that earning outside money may be a conflict of interest, so I formed a 12-piece band that would play for charity events. More on that later, for now a little more on "growing up."

Growing up on Brown Street, in a section of Little Italy, I went to St. Peter & Paul grammar school. I then attended St. Thomas the Apostle School until I started at Aquinas Institute, an All-Boys Catholic High School. I was a decent student, making the honor roll sometimes. When I was a junior, I won my first election, by popular vote, for Senior Student Council Secretary. That election experience was probably a foreshadowing of elections to come during my legal career.

Enjoying sports, I ran track and played basketball. In my Junior year, I believe there were over 1000 students enrolled at AQ and there were 12 spots on the Varsity basketball team. I was so excited as I seemed to be doing well at try-outs. They would post the fresh cuts from the team every day, and I made it to the last day of cuts. I ended up being the last boy cut. Looking back, although I was very disappointed, it was a good lesson in life.

Aquinas helped shaped me in more ways than one. I couldn't have asked for a better high school education and environment. I have friendships from Aquinas that I still cherish and enjoy.

One of my friends from Aquinas, Hank Jesserer, has been my friend through all of the benches I have sat on. I asked him to share a little of what that was like since we were just kids in high school when our friendship began. I thought he might have a unique perspective. So, now I will call to the stand my first Character Witness, Hank Jesserer:

"I have known Judge Joe Valentino since we graduated from high school. We both attended Aquinas Institute and have been friends for over 55 years. Our relationship is a comfortable one considering we have been through so many of life's stages together. I remember him marrying a beautiful woman from England, and they raised four great boys. That was essentially his personal life. Got married, stayed married, and raised four outstanding boys into men. That was a full-time job all by itself.

I watched Judge Valentino on the bench for many years. I was a lawyer practicing in all of the Courts of Monroe County and had first hand opportunities to see him. I observed Judge Valentino parcel justice to the individuals who appeared before him. Each person was always treated with respect and somehow, he found enough time for each person to feel like they were heard and a constructive part of the process.

In City Court, many cases and defendants are handled weekly. The charges are generally not serious, but they are critical as those are generally the first negative experience with the law for the defendant. The more positive the experience the less likely there would be other charges to come in the future. The large number of cases handled is a challenge to a Judge to do real justice to each case. Judge Valentino always handled his Court with dignity and patience.

I saw Justice Valentino in the Supreme Court where he handled more serious charges with more serious consequences. I was happy to see he was able to make the transition from City to Supreme Court, and he did not miss a step. I specifically remember him handling a case where the male defendant was accused of sexually abusing some little boys. Knowing the Judge had four boys at home, I knew this case must be difficult for him. I was so impressed with his fairness and impartiality in handling the issues that came up in that trial. Justice Valentino had the amazing ability to disassociate himself from the horror of the testimony that was before him. I don't think there is a defendant who appeared before him who didn't think he got a fair shot. That reminds me that when Justice Valentino was in the District Attorney's office he prosecuted a highly publicized rape case. There was a conviction and many years after the man was released from prison he saw Justice Valentino on the street. This man shook the Judge's hand and proceeded to tell him he had found God while in prison and was a reverend in his Church. That is the only time I am aware that a convicted defendant took the time to attempt to mend his fences with the prosecutor.

Justice Valentino also had the ability to use humor to defuse stressful situations and/or to remind everyone that no one is perfect. Justice Valentino is a man fully immersed in his community. He can't go anywhere without someone recognizing him and patting him on the back. There is no hiding that Justice Valentino is Monroe County's Man of La Mancha. He has struggled for so many years to bring Justice to our world.

When Justice Valentino is on the bench he is very serious and professional but there is another side where he is in the band known as Giuseppe' Scungili and the Screaming Seagull Revue. He always has a big smile on his face as he plays his guitar and sings the lyrics of a song. His band does not play for personal gain. They will only play where a charity will benefit from the proceeds of their work. Many of the charities that the band supports have the biggest fundraiser of the year on that night.

Justice Valentino is a multi-talented man who has found significant ways to give back to his fellow man and woman. Courtesy and respect are the words of the day and the life blood of the Judge."

In 2016, I was honored to be inducted to the Aquinas Hall of Fame. At the Induction Ceremony and Dinner, I shared a story about a formative occurrence in my life. My Geometry teacher gave us a take home test over the weekend. I didn't get a chance to do it (too busy), so I copied answers from a fellow student who had copied his answers from another student. The teacher noticed the three of us had the same answers and confronted us on Tuesday. I confessed that "I copied from a certain student." That student stated that he copied from another student. The priest called us up to the front of the class one at a time. The student who did no copying received one whack on the rear with a razor strop. The student I copied from received two whacks. Now this was Math class so I quickly formulated the consequences in my head which would be THREE whacks with the strop on the rear end for me. I learned a valuable lesson: Don't cheat! That includes copying homework from a friend.

I guess that was the seed for the honesty I have held onto consistently throughout my legal career. I have stressed honesty during professional mentoring of new lawyers and students as well as interacting with my peers. Integrity is most important. You are only as good as your word.

─────────────── **SIDEBAR** ───────────────

When I got caught cheating and received the whacks, my rear end was very sore. I had to sit down very carefully! But … there was no way that I would tell my dad at supper that night. I knew that he would be mad at me, would definitely side with the priest, and probably add some more punishment to an already sore rear end.

───────────────── ⇒•⇐ ─────────────────

I have been fortunate to have met some wonderful friends as a youth. Whether it was neighborhood kids, school mates, or summer camp mates, many are lasting friends even today. As an example, when I was only around 14 years old, I met one of my closest friends today, Tad Knight. My third son is named in honor of Tad.

I was proud to be the first Valentino to go to college. A priest from Aquinas took some AQ students on a college visit to Niagara University. I liked my visit to the college and I subsequently applied to admission there. English was my major because I wanted to be an English teacher and liked to write. It would be safe to say that I wasn't as good a student in college as I was in High School. Playing in a band came first, and going to class and studying were distant seconds.

Music was more or less my whole life while I was in college. I played the bass and joined a band, The Krax. We played at various clubs and beer blasts sometimes three or four times a week. We traveled around the area and we even opened for some pretty big names.

––––––––––––––– **SIDEBAR** –––––––––––––––

My friend was planning to go to law school after he graduated from Niagara. I didn't know what I was going to do, but the idea of law school intrigued me. I decided to take the LSAT and see how I would do.

The night before the LSAT, we opened for the Box Tops in Buffalo. I struggled to get out of bed the next morning to drive to the exam which was back in Buffalo! I almost decided to stay in bed. (a little too much partying the previous night). I ended up doing well on the LSAT and went to law school.

St. John's University Law School, at that time located in Brooklyn New York, was where I attended law school. The lure to NYC was definitely the most contributing factor in that decision. The prospect of playing music in the Big Apple was exciting. Turns out that I underestimated how much work law school would be and my music aspirations quickly took a back seat to my academics.

Law School was where I had to build study habits as I had virtually no solid study habits in college! Law School was difficult for me. I had a great deal of help from my three roommates the first year. I also had some very interesting law school professors. It was important to soak up the knowledge from the likes of Mario Cuomo, former governor of New York. When I became a City Court Judge, he sent me a congratulatory letter that I still have today. I remember a couple of other professors—one who allegedly represented Marilyn Monroe in her divorce proceedings and one who allegedly was a consultant for the Perry Mason Show on TV.

ROTC was also a part of my law school experience. Many of the first-year students received a draft notice right after college graduation, me included. I went down to the local draft office, and explained that I was supposed to go to Law School in September. The woman at the desk barely looked up "You'll be gone by January." I wasn't sure if she meant from school or from this earth. I realized that if I went into the Army at that time, then I probably would have never returned to Law School. So, I signed up for Army ROTC at St. John's. You can imagine fifty lawyers in one unit.

As graduation approached, I was prepared to go on active duty as an Infantry Officer. My active duty lasted only four months at Ft. Benning, Georgia because there was a Reduction in Force as the Vietnam War was ending. I had to join the US Army Reserves, however. While I was in the Reserves,

I was hired to be an Assistant DA. I was told by my Colonel that the ADA job was one that qualified for a law enforcement deferment. I applied. About a month later, I received a package in the mail from St. Louis, Missouri ... I was sure it was my release papers. Instead it was a promotion to Captain!

In the spirit of full disclosure, I believe that I have provided you with all relevant evidence (that I can remember!) referencing the formation of my character in this Pre-Trial Discovery proceeding.

CHAPTER II

OPENING STATEMENTS

My legal career began in 1973 as an associate attorney with the law firm of Palmiere, Passero and Crimi. It was a great place to start, and I was fortunate to have such good mentors who taught me so much about the law and how to conduct myself in the courtroom.

My first interview during the hiring process was with Ronnie Passero. He was very kind to me and seemed interested. I then had a second interview with all the partners in Charlie Crimi's office. When I walked into the office, the first thing I saw on the wall was Charlie's appointment document signed by Attorney General Robert Kennedy. I was quite impressed. After the interview, I was asked to join the firm.

All three partners were great teachers. Ronnie Passero became my "practical civil law" teacher concerning wills, real estate closings and civil law suits. He was especially good at teaching me how to deal with insurance companies. Norman Palmiere taught me the things about a legal career that they don't necessarily teach you in Law School, like how to be a businessman. He wanted me to see the attorney/client relationship from beginning to end and invited me to sit in with a new client. After the initial meeting when he discussed his fee with the client, I asked him about it. How did he know what to charge? *(They don't teach you that in Law School!).* Norman showed me a picture of his family that he had on his desk. He said that whenever he was going to present a fee, he looked at the photo. He knew he had to ask for a sufficient fee to take care of his family. That always stuck with me. I channeled right into criminal law. Charlie Crimi always took the time to answer my questions and guide me through "young lawyer stumbles." We would have case meetings on Fridays and I will never forget Charlie's insight, but most of all, his humor during those meetings

For my first trial, I was assigned to represent a kid who had allegedly stolen some drywall. The witness's account could be damaging because he said he had heard the details of the crime while he was cleaning in his role as a janitor. I noticed that the ADA stood right in front of the witness and talked loudly and slowly. When it was my turn to question the witness, I faced the judge, not even looking at the witness. When the witness didn't answer the question asked, I repeated it, again not facing the witness. It was clear that the witness couldn't hear me and if he couldn't hear me, how could he have heard the details of the crime? The alleged thief was found not guilty, and I felt a little like Perry Mason. I was hooked on trial work from that point on. Unfortunately for the defendant, he was arrested on another charge as he left the Hall of Justice!

As time progressed, the partners in the firm under-stood my love of the courtroom. They said that I could always return to the firm, but if I wanted to get a great deal of trial experience, I should apply to work in either the Public Defender's Office or the District Attorney's Office. It would be a "baptism by fire." I would then be an experienced trial attorney and more valuable to the law firm. They also thought that I would get a better understanding of how the police worked and how to pick a jury. Norman and Charlie were prosecutors in their early careers so they encouraged me to go into the DA's Office. They helped me with my application and were much more than passive references. I was chosen and eight others with me. There was a special funding given by President Nixon at the time to beef up DA Offices around the country, which undoubtedly helped also.

--------------------- **SIDEBAR** ---------------------

My "office" (desk) at Palmiere, Passero and Crimi was in the law library. When I arrived at the DA's office I was led to my new "office"—a desk in the DA's law library!

CHAPTER III

DISTRICT ATTORNEY'S OFFICE

—————◦—————

I transitioned into the DA's Office pretty quickly. Because of my defense experience in private practice, I was allowed to skip prosecuting cases in City Court and went right to felonies. Within my first year I was given my first murder trial. A file was given to me by a more experienced ADA. "This is a good case for you try." I didn't know that I should have been leery of those words. My first murder trial involved two drug dealers. They were having a shootout with the victim and the only witnesses were two prostitutes. Neither witness was reliable; they were both high on heroin on the night of the murder.

One was so high on heroin during the trial, that she fell asleep on the stand. The other was waiting in my office to testify. She kept trying to leave so the only way that two of my fellow ADAs could keep her in the office was to turn on the radio and let her dance on my desk. When she finally got on the stand, she described the assailants fleeing quickly and running from the scene. One of the defendants had a discernible limp and couldn't have even walked quickly from the scene. Needless to say, "Not Guilty" was the jury's verdict.

Another case that stood out to me from my early ADA years, was a rape case involving a teenage girl victim. As we were preparing for trial I felt like there was some hesitation on her part—like I wasn't getting the full extent of what truly had happened. I asked to speak with her without her parents and asked her again if there was anything else that I needed to know about that night. I was glad I pressed the issue, because she was embarrassed to let her parents know that she actually had a beer that night. Her parents were very understanding when we all talked about it. That fact obviously didn't negate the rape at all, and I was happy that we got everything out in the open. By the time we reached the trial, she could talk freely about it. The rapist was convicted. As a point of interest in the case, the Sheriff's Office got a tip that the offender was going to be at a local concert, and they brought the victim with them. The police walked with her while she viewed row after row after row of filled seats. She ultimately picked him out of the crowd. It was probably the biggest line up in history.

There was another trial for robbery. The suspect robbed a store in a ski mask. I really didn't have a whole lot of hard evidence, and the victim could only identify the robber by his teeth. The defendant was convicted, but the conviction was later overturned by the Appellate Division, citing not enough evidence to convict. I called the defense lawyer and congratulated him on the decision. He laughed and wanted to know why I was congratulating him … his guy had been convicted without any evidence!

As the years went on, I was promoted to the head of the Career Criminal Bureau. It was a great concept in the prosecution of repeat offenders. I was fortunate to have two good attorneys and two very sharp investigators in the bureau. Later, I was promoted to the Chief Attorney of Major Crimes prosecution.

A case that made its mark on me, and of great interest to the Rochester community, was a highly publicized Rape Case. A teacher had been sexually assaulted in a Parking Garage. Due to poor lighting in the garage, there were numerous assaults around that time.

The police investigators worked tirelessly and finally they had a suspect. The victim had indicated that her attacker had a reddish tint to his afro. When the police went to the suspect's home to ask a few questions, his relatives let them in as he was not home. While they were in the living room, the defendant walked through the front door. The sun shining behind him revealed a reddish tint in his hair.

At the trial, the defendant produced an alibi. He also testified that the sex was consensual as he indicated that they were lovers.

During cross-examination, I asked the defendant if he could describe the victim's apartment and her bed. On rebuttal, I brought in witnesses to show that his description of the apartment was obviously incorrect and that her bed was a waterbed and NOT a "normal bed" as he had earlier described.

After the defendant was convicted, his father approached me in the hallway. He told me the Bible says that God delivers justice through the angels of the Lord, and he was an angel of God. A time later, the father came to the DA's Office and apologized for what he had said. He explained how upset he was and felt sorry for the threat. I understood his emotional attack on me; the poor father was so grief stricken by the trial.

About a month after the trial, the victim also came to the DA's Office. She gave me a beautiful wax rendition of the St. George Medallion that she had made herself. St. George was the slayer of dragons, she said, and so she thought I should have it. I still have it today. I have received many personal gifts such as this through the years. I have kept them all.

Wax Medallion of St. George slaying the Dragon.

As a sequel to this story, many, many years later, this particular defendant was released from prison. I was on Monroe Avenue and this guy, across the street, turned toward me and ran to me. He stood in front of me and asked if I knew who he was. I wasn't sure at first, but then I slowly recognized him. He stated that he had found God in prison, was now a minister, and his life was on the right path. I congratulated him and then I breathed a quiet sigh of relief as he crossed the street.

———✦———

I was in the DA's Office for 8½ years. It was a great learning experience, not just about the law and trial work, but also about people.

As earlier indicated, I held various positions while in the DA's Office. My last administrative position there was as the Special Assistant in charge of all Local Courts (City, Town and Village Courts). It was a good experience as I learned all about the local courts and met and befriended many of their personnel. I also enjoyed teaching young, new ADAs. I was also appointed by the DA to be his Representative to the Monroe County Community Service Sentencing Project. Prior to 1980, Community Service wasn't used as an alternative sentence. The Panel garnered support from the ADAs, League of Woman Voters, Sheriff's Office and others. Happy to sit on the panel, I believed then, and still do today, that it is better to get those convicted of larcenous crimes working rather than sitting in jail.

The DA also named me the Liaison to the Rochester Police Department Sections and the DA's representative to the City's Neighborhood Association Meetings. I got the nickname, "Cardinal Richeleau" by the DA Office Administrator, as I was often sent out to answer questions pertaining to the DA's Office and to calm people who may be frustrated or angry with the Criminal Justice System.

I had many interesting cases while I served as an Assistant District Attorney. No doubt the highest profiled case I tried was the case of the nun accused of killing her baby. After the trial, a book by Catherine Breslin, called *Unholy Child*, was written and later the movie, *Agnes of God*, was released. Both the book and the movie were categorized as fiction. Both were about this case, but differed somewhat from the events that actually occurred in and out of trial. As I was reflecting on this case, I thought the personal reflections I had may be interesting. I am sharing a narrative of my perceptions during that trial. Some names and places have been changed.

ARE YOU SITTING DOWN?

The phone is ringing.

I roll over and see that it is 6:00 AM. There are no "good" phone calls this early in the morning.

"Hello?"

"Joe, this is the DA. Sorry if I woke you up. We have a situation."

The Monroe County District Attorney calling at 6:00 AM would not be unusual if I was on call. I was not.

"It's okay … I'm up … What is it?"

"Well, I realize that you are not on call. (Uh oh … not good.) We had another ADA at the scene of a possible homicide overnight, but he needs help. I want you to take over and assist the police."

"Where do you want me to go? What's the story?"

"Are you sitting down?"

Strange question …

"I would like you to go to the Convent in Brighton and …"

"No? A nun was killed?"

"Well the police believe that a baby was killed. Can you get there soon? I have some of the info, but it's better if you get going. They will fill you in on all of the details when you get there."

"Uh … yeah … okay … I'll be there as soon as I can."

Quietly I shave, shower, dress and am ready to go. Janet was not quite awake. As I was about to go downstairs, I heard her ask, "Where are you going so early?"

"Are you sitting down?" began my narrative. I quickly told her before I left.

It was a twenty-five minute drive to the convent. As I pulled into the parking lot, it struck me that I had never been in a convent in my life. There were police in the entranceway to the building. I walked through the open door. It was quiet and still except for the faint sound of sobbing coming from one of the far away rooms. The police seemed happy to see me. The Assistant DAs who were called to homicide scenes in those days knew that they were often asked to stay in the background and only to assist the police on legal issues. I sensed that they wanted a little more from me that morning.

I could see three or four policemen sitting down on chairs interviewing different women. Are they nuns? Yes, I'm pretty sure they are, but not dressed as I remembered from grammar school. I listen to their quiet narratives. After hearing pieces of conversation, it was evident that a baby was found in a bedroom. I asked one of the nuns "Who is the Mother Superior here?" One of them stood up and stated that was not the title anymore, but explained that she was in charge. As she approached me, I saw she had been crying. She introduced herself and I immediately thought she seemed younger than the rest. She had a somewhat blank, yet pained look on her face. A look that revealed her discomfort at having all these strange people in her house. These people were asking so many questions. When I introduced myself as an Assistant District Attorney, the tears began to fall again. I reached into my pocket and then gave her my handkerchief.

Years later, I was at a Parish Council meeting. The Pastor asked if I had met the new School Principal yet. I turned and a smiling Sister greeted me. It was the "Mother Superior"! She stated that she knew that I would be at the meeting and she had something for me ... It was my handkerchief!

_____ ——›•‹—— _____

I asked to see the room where the baby was found. She led me down a hallway lined with doors. It looked very similar to a college dorm. She really didn't have to point out the room as I realized it was the one where the police congregated. The familiar evidence tape seemed so foreign in this setting. I looked in from the hallway. There was a bed, a desk and a bookcase. It was stark.

"Is there any problem if I look around?"

"No problem. It's been photographed, dusted and evidence collected. The nuns found the baby in a wastebasket, behind that kitty corner bookcase."

I walked into the room alone. My shoes seemed to be too loud on this tile floor. To my surprise, I spied a wastebasket by the desk *(can't be the same one...)*. I noticed that inside of the basket was a color photo torn into pieces. Realizing that the basket containing the baby had to have been collected as evidence, I picked up this different basket and dumped the pieces onto the floor. As I put the "puzzle" together, slowly a color photo of a young woman emerged. I was twenty-nine years old then and she looked my age. She looked healthy and she was smiling. Sobbing filled the room and I realized that Sister Ann Marie was standing behind me.

As we walked back to the living room area, I started to contemplate the enormity of the situation. A nun gave birth to a baby in that room. The baby is dead. So many questions ...

The lieutenant was on the phone. "The baby is at the M.E.'s Office. Preliminarily, they think it may be a homicide. Yeah, I know. Could be panties and some other material forced down the baby's throat."

This is going to be a long day. Little did I know that the day would turn into long months and then a very intense trial.

PRE-TRIAL ISSUES

As the preparations progressed for the case, there was a Pre-Trial that left me feeling like a couple of bombs went off. As I remember it happening ...

I better get moving. It's Friday morning with the last Pre-Trial Conference before Jury selection on Monday. The Judge's door is open. His secretary smiles and nods for me to go inside. As I walk into his chambers, I see that Charlie Crimi, attorney for the Defendant and the attorney for the Diocese of Rochester are already seated. The judge is behind his desk and as always, is pleasant. We exchange greetings as I sit down. The judge then asks for information concerning procedures, times, etc. After about five minutes, the first "bomb" is dropped:

"Openings shouldn't take all morning, right gentlemen? Joe, make sure that you have witnesses ready to go on Monday." The judge stated as an aside as he shuffled through some papers.

It didn't register at first. Jury selection was scheduled for Monday morning. My witnesses arc scheduled to come to Court later in the week as I was anticipating two or three days for Jury selection.

"Judge, Jury selection is Monday morning. How can ..."

"Joe, they want to go Bench with no Jury.

"I was not aware of that."

"In any event, your witnesses must be ready on Monday."

Countless hours of jury selection preparation, and the order of witnesses scheduled to testify were formulated to give a chronological explanation to the jury of how the defendant is guilty beyond a reasonable doubt. I harbored a fear, but also a sincere hope, that there would be no problem. The witnesses will be ready to go on Monday! Needless to say, the conference began with a rattled prosecutor.

All other discussions progressed smoothly until ...

When evidentiary matters were being discussed, it was stated that the defense intended to present evidence that any sexual intercourse was nonconsensual.

"Do you mean that she was raped?" I asked in disbelief.

"We mean that it was nonconsensual."

As the evidence in this case unfolded, I determined that there was no need to discuss the sexual intercourse at trial. I felt that it was irrelevant to the crime charged. Our investigation clearly showed that there was no rape. There was absolutely no evidence, that we were aware, of forcible intercourse. No evidence from the baby's father, no evidence from the mother's statements and no evidence from other witnesses. Also, we excluded the father as an accomplice to the homicide as it was verified that the father, who was a railroad employee, was many, many miles away when the baby was born and subsequently found dead.

"There is no evidence of a rape here. There was no rape." I continued ..."Judge, we do not intend to present any proof concerning the father of the baby. His identity is irrelevant to this trial, and we do not intend to call him as a witness. The attorneys know, through discovery, the circumstances surrounding the intercourse. There was no rape. However, if the defense intends to offer proof concerning a rape, we would then call the father as a witness, in rebuttal, to prove consensual intercourse. And we will call other witnesses to show consent."

The room was silent for a few seconds. Charlie, who had been somewhat quiet all morning, spoke up:

"Judge, the attorney for the Diocese and I may discuss this matter further, but I realize that because the trial is starting Monday, in the interest of fairness and cooperation that has been the norm on both sides, there should be no surprises. Therefore, we can indicate to you, at this time, that the defense will not be introducing any evidence concerning the father of the baby, or any evidence, for that matter, concerning sexual intercourse."

Both men were very good trial attorneys. The Diocesan Attorney, a former successful prosecutor himself, was also polite and always a gentleman. I personally did not know him very well before this trial.

I did know Charlie Crimi. Articulate, intelligent, kind and witty, he was truly someone that a 30-year-old Assistant DA would respect and try to emulate. I can tell you that I had a history of "looking up to him." As you have read in this book, he was my first boss. As a brand new attorney in his firm, I was very, very green … all ears and eyes … I learned from Charlie. He was my mentor, and now I was his opponent. This irony was not lost on me.

The Judge quickly seized on Charlie's words:

"Okay. Now that we've settled that, is there anything else to discuss?"

The Defense Attorneys indicated that they had nothing more and Charlie gave me a warm, knowing smile as he got up to leave.

We all thanked the Judge and left his Chambers. The DA's Office, at that time, was on the same floor as the County Courts in the Hall of Justice. Many thoughts filled my mind as I slowly walked to my office. But one thought brought a smile to my face …

"Charlie was smart to pull back. He is a good lawyer."

INNER THOUGHTS AT TRIAL

There are no open seats in the courtroom. It's filled with reporters, attorneys, police, nuns and many interested people from near and far, even as far as Los Angeles. In the weeks leading up to the trial, the DA's Office received many letters from all over the world. The story captured the interest of many. The courtroom began to "buzz," so I realized that the defendant had arrived. She came into Court between her two attorneys. She was very thin … very pale … and frail. The three sat at the opposite Counsel table.

"All rise." And the trial began.

Opening statements first. Then the steady stream of witnesses … testifying nuns, policemen, and doctors. Summations and many legal arguments and issues. Those were tough days and tough nights.

The Defendant took the stand. Oftentimes, she was so quiet in her speech, I strained to hear her.

She attempted to explain certain facts previously discussed in the trial:

- The constant denial of her pregnancy to everyone, even to the doctors at the hospital emergency department.

- Her "plan" concerning the birth of the baby (which did not reflect her actions surrounding that occurrence.)

And, most of all, was what I termed her "amnesia by convenience" when it came to the most compelling evidence: the newborn baby stuffed in a wastebasket, behind a bookcase.

My memory of the trial contains a whirlwind of images. I felt a sense of relief at the end of the trial when I stated, "The People rest."

From the beginning, I believed that my duty in this case was to present all the evidence to a jury. They would have had the responsibility to determine Guilty or Not Guilty. Now all was placed before the Judge in this Bench Trial and he had the ultimate responsibility.

After all proof was closed, the defense argued a motion to dismiss the charges against the defendant claiming that I had not proved that the baby was born alive. We clearly rebutted that argument relying on two major points revealed at the autopsy:

1. The baby's lungs floated on water indicating an air flow in the lungs.

2. Even more compelling, there was petechial hemorrhaging around the baby's eyes indicating a live

person and signs of asphyxia caused by some external means of airway obstruction.

As the prosecutor, I argued that both matters of proof, taken together, proved that the baby, before it was strangled, was an independent, self-breathing, living human being.

The Judge did not dismiss the charges after the Motion argument.

He stepped down to deliberate and consider all the evidence and applicable law before reaching a verdict.

When the Court reconvened for the verdict, I was unusually calm. Normally, I would have been nervous. It is very tense in the courtroom when there is a verdict announced. I did not feel tense at that time.

In my mind, I surmised that the compassionate judge may not find the defendant guilty of Manslaughter, but instead guilty of the lesser included offense of Criminally Negligent Homicide. Furthering that manner of thought, I did not entirely rule out a Not Guilty verdict.

When the judge came to the bench, the first thing he did was give me a compliment. He stated that I presented myself very professionally with attorney skills beyond my years. (The kiss of death before a Bench Trial verdict!!)

"Not Guilty of Manslaughter. Not Guilty of Criminally Negligent Homicide."

He rose and left the Courtroom.

I heard gasps and quiet crying in the courtroom.

As I indicated, the verdict, itself, was not entirely a surprise to me.

I stood up, started to collect my notes, and felt one of the other Assistant DAs come to my side. I realized that he was there to stand by me and to lift my spirits. In actuality, there was no disappointment. I felt that I had done my job in the best way possible in presenting all of the evidence. I shook Charlie's hand. The Diocesan Attorney was in the process of ushering the defendant out of the courtroom. It was my last glimpse of the defendant.

At various times in the courtroom, I would look over to the defense table. When she was on the witness stand, her eyes met mine quite often. During the entire trial, I never saw any discernible emotional reaction from her.

The defendant and I walked the same path out of the courtroom that day.

Actually, we were both free. I was free from the all the hard work and stress that had emanated from the trial. She was free from the burden of a homicide charge.

Both of us free ... except for the memory.

———————

You can see being in the DA's office had some ups and downs, but it was the people in the office that helped make the job even more of a pleasure. One of those people was Bruce Goldman. As Character Witness #2, Bruce shares a little about our relationship, what the DA's office was like and the friendship we have had ever since.

"My first interaction with Joseph Daniel Valentino occurred long before I actually met him. My dad used to get his haircut at Joseph's father's barber shop on Joseph Avenue in the City of Rochester. At those events the two fathers would chat about their respective sons and their activities. After I became a teenager my dad would take me along to get my hair cut at the barber shop and that is where I met Joe's dad Nick. It was easy to see why he and my dad got along because they were both really good persons. Their personalities were so similar. That was a portent of what was to come when Joe and I met and became friends. We didn't fall too far from our respective paternal trees.

Years later, after Joe and I had finished our educations in undergraduate and then law school, we met in early 1972. We immediately hit it off. We were both employed in different small private law offices. We were always being sent to court by the senior attorneys in our offices to ask for continuances of their cases because they didn't want to make the appearance. After a while, Joe and I agreed that the two of us were the best adjourners in town.

Our friendship continued, and in early 1974 we were united in the same law practice as we both joined the Monroe County District Attorney's Office under District Attorney Jack Lazarus. Needless to say, both of our fathers were ecstatic about this development and were beaming with great pride about their sons' new adventures in their careers. Working daily with Joe we had great contact with each other. We worked very hard, but we played very hard too. We had some great colleagues, and the environment lent itself to some incremental increases in our professional legal abilities. It was at this time that I began to realize one of Joe's great qualities. He was one of the fairest persons that I had ever seen.

Our job description in the District Attorney's Office was to seek justice. Many citizens think that the job simply requires convicting people and placing them in jail. The caption of any accusatory instrument really defines what our job was. The caption always read "The People of the State of New York versus..." The People means everyone. It means those who have been aggrieved by crime as well as those charged with a crime. Those charged with a crime have to be prosecuted in a fair and just manner. Joe embodied that concept.

Years later when he left the District Attorney's Office to become a member of the judiciary, Judge Joseph Daniel Valentino continued that thought process at every level of the court system that he served in. People were treated with dignity, and cases handled by him always bore the trademark of a fair process. He was the fairest judge that I ever appeared before and even if I would disagree with him I knew that I had been given a fair hearing of my point of view.

Now that both of us are retired we still spend great times together playing golf and enjoying lunches with our many buddies. He is still the fairest person that I know, and we both enjoy reminiscing about our many stories that occurred during our careers."

CHAPTER IV

CITY COURT

After spending 8½ years in the District Attorney's Office, I was appointed by Mayor Thomas Ryan to Rochester City Court in late December of 1982. I was to begin sitting on the bench on the first court day in January 1983. There would be no Judge School for me before my first day. It would be trial by fire, and I was hoping for the best.

I still had to run for election in 1983 which would be my first successful foray into politics. I will share the details of "running for election" a little later.

Enthusiastic and wet behind the ears, my first courtroom experience involved some laughter. I was presiding over arraignments and Dan Mastrella was the Asst. DA present in court. On my first one, I read the complaint, presumably to the defendant. I then asked Mr. Mastrella how he was going to plead after reading the charges. Mr. Mastrella politely said, "I don't know how I am going to plea Judge, but you might want to ask the defendant." Nothing like a little levity to start your judicial career.

I have often been asked, "What's it like being a judge?" or "What went through your mind when you first became a judge?" I must admit that it was a little overwhelming at first. Everyone was so  nice to me in City Court. I was taken to my Chambers which is a great English Common Law word for the judge's office, the secretary's office, the waiting area, and the best part ... the judge's bathroom. Yes, my own bathroom!!! (It really wasn't until I hit 60 years old did I fully appreciate that amenity.)

I remember putting my robe on over my suit coat the first day of Court. "No, that's not going to work." I quickly learned that the suit coat always comes off. I walked into the courtroom to hear, "All Rise, Court is in session. The Honorable Joseph D. Valentino presiding." Gulp! That's me! I started to walk up the stairs and I had to do something that I imagine judges, and wearers of long dresses, have been doing for years, I had to grab the side of my robe and pull it up so that I didn't step on it. Needless to say, through the years I tripped once and awhile.

The attorneys lined up for applications, that is, they wanted to call their cases. They often have cases in other courtrooms, so it is a good procedure to allow them to make applications on behalf of their clients. Some of the attorneys congratulated me. I noticed that all of the attorneys were very respectful. I thought about that during the day and came to the realization that they were respecting the robes and the bench which are the symbols of justice. It wasn't the guy in the robes … not yet at least … I was going to have to earn their respect.

It was the first day of 33 years on the bench. I can honestly say that, although some days were stressful and filled with difficult decisions, I loved presiding over cases in the courtroom. I loved the drama of the jury trial, the challenge of evidentiary questions, and most of all, the learning experience. What was it like being a judge? It was the greatest experience, and I was so very fortunate to be Judge Valentino for all those years.

There were many moments in City Court that were more serious than my first arraignment.

One decision while I was on the City Court bench garnered national attention. The Police Department often conducted Prostitution Raids throughout the city. At that time, for a prostitute to be released, one condition was a mandatory physical examination to check for diseases. Seemed like a reasonable enough practice.

There were "John" raids, too. I noticed that when the Johns (the patrons) were released they did not have the same requirement to have a physical. That didn't seem right to me. They would be just as responsible for passing on diseases, so I ordered physicals for all the Johns, too. That created quite an uproar. Some lawyers and judges thought it was not a good idea, but I held my ground. It made sense to me and now it has become common practice. Interestingly, there was an article about my decision in *Ms. Magazine!* This practice was recognized and featured in the November 1983 issue.

Another precedent setting trial I had was about computer fraud. The defendant, skilled on the computer, was angry because he was fired from his job. He subsequently issued commands to his company's computer software which took the computers off their normal course of action. He was prosecuted under a fairly recent NYS Penal Law statute making computer tampering a crime. The defense made legal motions asking for a dismissal, indicating that his actions were not illegal under the statute. I denied the motion as I felt that the defendant's actions fell squarely within the meaning of the statute defining computer tampering. He was found guilty and appealed to the state's Appellate Courts. My decision was affirmed all the way up, and once again I found myself cited in a national magazine! This time concerning computer fraud and tampering.

I was fortunate to have many interesting City Court legal matters. In one case, the defendant may have made threats during a combative phone call that was initiated by someone else. I ruled that the defendant could not be prosecuted for aggravated harassment because she did not initiate the phone call. The brief written by the defense attorney was excellent, and I believe that this ruling is still "good law" today.

In another case, three nuns were leading (and singing!) a demonstration at a government office voicing concern over an identification practice used by Monroe County Social Services. (...nuns...again!!) The three nuns considered this practice unfair and discriminatory. Prior to the trial, the defense attorney made a motion to seat a jury consisting of all Rochester City residents. His argument was actually a challenge to the jury pool because the jurors were drawn from the entire county instead of only the city where the defendants were charged. There were various points to this challenge, but the two that I found most relevant were that, first, had the defendants been charged in any of the Towns in Monroe County, the jury pool would have consisted of that Towns' residents only, and second, distinct minority groups were underrepresented in the jury pool for City Court cases. I sustained the challenge and a jury pool of only City of Rochester residents were brought to the courtroom. When I took the bench for jury selection, I looked out into the courtroom and saw the most diverse prospective jury pool I had ever seen in my years as a judge. No one has challenged this decision in Monroe County and the Commissioner of Jurors tells me that, to this day, if an all-City jury pool is requested by either party, he will cooperate with this request.

⟶•⟵

As an aside, one of the pleasures I had during my time in City Court, was teaching and mentoring students at Rochester Institute of Technology. In 1984, an RIT professor approached me about creating a Criminal Justice Internship Program. That program became accredited in the Criminal Justice Program and most of the students that utilized the program were interested in law enforcement or pre-law. We placed students in City, County and Supreme Courts. They also got some experience in Family Court, Drug Court, and the diversion courts. Where they went next depended on their interests that I would discern from the conversations we had during my open-door policy. At the end of the day, the interns could come in and discuss anything they wanted to talk about. I was very proud of this program.

The internship program sparked a great relationship with RIT and in 1985 I was asked to be an adjunct professor in the Criminal Justice Department. In any class that I taught, the students were required to spend ten hours in a courtroom, where I felt they would have a real criminal justice experience and not just a learning experience from me or their books.

I spent 30 years as an adjunct professor and really enjoyed it. I developed different courses over the years, but a favorite was COURTS. In this class, the students were given a fact pattern of an actual trial where I had previously presided. I would bring in many of the people involved in the case ... the ADA, Defense Attorney, DNA expert, Medical Examiner ... to name a few. They would provide insights and answer questions from the students. I thought it was very important for them to really understand the trial experience. It was always one of the more popular classes and often attended by students NOT enrolled in the class!

RIT was not my only teaching gig through the years. I "guest-lectured" at just about every college in the area and at Syracuse Law School. I also taught Identification Procedures at the NYS Police and Rochester Police Academies. When I was the Drug Court Judge, I went with Judge Schwartz all over the USA and often presented lectures, especially for the NY State Drug Court Association.

When I went to college, I was an English major with the thought of becoming a teacher someday. So, there always was a down-deep desire to be a teacher. I am very fortunate that I was able to also achieve this goal in my life.

CHAPTER V

DRUG TREATMENT COURT

———··◦··———

It was Christmas time, 1996. I received a call from Judge John Schwartz. He wanted to meet with me to discuss a "court matter."

As indicated earlier in this book, I had recently written that court decision indicating that a defendant in the City Court of Rochester was entitled to have a jury composed of City of Rochester residents. I was fairly certain that Judge Schwartz wanted to talk to me about this decision. I was mistaken.

Judge John Schwartz had started this new program, The Rochester Drug Treatment Court, and it was just about two years old. It was a new concept and the first Drug Court in New York State. The bottom line was that it united the court system with substance abuse institutions and their substance abuse treatment employees. I, like many other judges working daily in the criminal courts, was somewhat skeptical of this "hybrid court." I was well aware that "revolving door justice" was prevalent in the way convicted addicts were handled in our courts, but I was not entirely convinced that this new court was the answer. Watching from afar, I was somewhat interested, but not enthusiastic.

However, I did admire Judge Schwartz concerning his persistence in the face of adversity. He fended off attacks from government officials, political party heads and from some of his fellow judges. These factions openly tried to stop him, but he forged on and gradually built this court with enduring determination.

When I walked into the room to meet Judge Schwartz, he was standing with the Chief Administrator of the Drug Court. That, in itself, should have given me fair warning! After introductions and "How are you?" niceties, Judge Schwartz began with an explanation that his dream was to institutionalize the Drug Treatment Court. He did not want it to be perceived as "Judge Schwartz's Drug Court," and he felt that to achieve this goal other judges would have to preside in that court. He then stated that I would be the best judge to "take over" this duty. (A masterful Judge Schwartz ego stroke!)

"Thank you for the compliment, John, but I am not interested," was my immediate reply. I loved presiding over jury trials which are the essence of our justice system. There were no jury trials in Drug Court. There were no trials of any kind in Drug Court! It was not for me.

True to form, he persisted. "Have you ever watched what happens in Drug Court?" he asked. I had never been in Drug Court. I didn't have the heart to tell him that I was not yet a "firm believer" in the effectiveness of the court at that point in time. He suggested that I stop in one morning soon and observe the court. He also suggested that I attend the upcoming "graduation" of those defendants who managed successfully to complete the entire program. I asked what that entailed. Seeing that he piqued my interest, he enthusiastically outlined the requirements of the contract that they sign before they can enter the Drug Court:

1. Staying crime and drug free for one year

2. Completing high school or obtaining a G.E.D.

3. Either having a job or going on to college

He indicated that the defendants understood that if they failed any one of these requirements, they are sentenced to jail. No probation and no community service. They would go directly to jail. If they agree, they must plead guilty to the crime charged. If they are successful, there would be no jail cell waiting for them, and the conviction may possibly be erased from their record.

He then was happy to add that The Chief Judge of the State of New York, at that time, Judith Kaye was scheduled to preside at the graduation. That was impressive in itself.

I agreed to observe the Drug Court proceedings mainly due to his exuberance! After observing one session, my interest was now even more piqued. I observed a second session, and it was becoming clear to me that this was a worthwhile innovation in Criminal Justice. These defendants had to answer to the judge, as in all courtrooms, but they also had to cooperate fully with all aspects of their treatment and answer to their treatment workers.

Another observation that was interesting was the discovery that the Rochester Police Department referred defendants to the court. Yes, you read that right, the police. I found that the police were one of the first organizations to understand the benefit of the drug court to the community. Realizing that the court made a concentrated effort to not accept the drug dealers, they supported the effort to try to get the addicts drug and crime free and back to being productive members of society.

The graduation ceremony was the final step needed to push me into acceptance of Judge Schwartz's offer. There were smiling "graduates" sitting in the courtroom beaming with pride. When receiving their certificate of graduation, some thanked the police officers present in the courtroom for arresting them! Some told of their difficult past, how they now have a future AND a future with no jail time. I could only think of how much they must differ from possible co-defendants who choose jail over participation in the drug court.

During one emotional narrative, I glanced over at the Chief Judge who was obviously moved by the defendants' stories. When Judge Kaye spoke to the courtroom she praised these men and women. While she spoke, it occurred to me that these defendants actually made a tough decision to go the difficult route of Drug Court. They could have pled guilty and served their time in jail and gotten it "over with" so to speak. Instead these defendants decided to stop using. They decided to become clean and coherent. They decided to get their families back. They decided on ultimate freedom, rather than life imprisonment by drug use.

That night I discussed Judge Schwartz's proposal extensively with my wife, Janet, as I did concerning all major decisions in my life. I told her about my observations and the graduation. She commented on the importance of this program to society, and that she realized the impact this court would have on my outlook concerning my work as a judge. "You would be the best pick for this job," she stated smiling. (I wondered if there was some sort of conspiracy involving her and Judge Schwartz? HA!) The next day I met with Judge Schwartz and asked, "When do I start?" Smiling, but showing no surprise, he stated "The beginning of the new year."

As they say, the rest is history. I was the presiding judge in the Rochester Drug Treatment Court from 1997 to the end of 2001, when I was elected to the New York State Supreme Court. The Drug Court was definitely a most fulfilling experience. For the first time as a judge, I felt that I was a positive influence on the lives of defendants who came before me. I felt that I was a contributing part of the criminal justice system. I can say today, without equivocation, that the Drug Courts, now numbering in the thousands in the USA and other countries, are positively the most praiseworthy and most valuable programs in our courts.

It will be a pleasure to share with you some of the humorous moments during my stay in the Drug Treatment Court in a later chapter, I Lost My Hair, But Not My Humor.

 SIDEBAR

I was the Drug Treatment Court Judge for five years. It was not unusual for me to be out and about and have someone approach me and hold up their hand with their fingers extended. That signified how many months or years that person had stayed sober. They would be so proud and it made me smile.

Drug Court worked for a variety of reasons, but I came to understand that no one sets out to be an addict. Sometimes

life circumstances take a direction that a person doesn't expect and they often deserve mercy and help getting sober. But, more often than not, they also need serious court intervention. If nothing else Drug Court was an accountability partner of sorts for them. I was also proud that during my time as the Drug Court Judge we saved numerous babies from being "crack babies." It is wonderful that those fifty babies were given a chance to someday become productive citizens in this community.

Just like I was a little reluctant to preside in Drug Treatment Court in the beginning, so was my Court Deputy, John Crespo. I think we both were pleasantly surprised at how meaningful DTC was and were happy we ended up there. Here is a little of what Character Witness John Crespo had to say about our time together:

> "It was sometime in 1996, I believe, when I was first made aware that I was going to be assigned to work with City Court Judge Joseph D. Valentino. The word on the street was that his deputy wanted a transfer out and nobody wanted in. "What the heck did I do to deserve this?" I asked myself. Who is this Joseph D. Valentino and most importantly, WHY ME? The more I inquired, the more vague the answers I got were. I've had my share of unpleasant assignments but never with a judge nobody wanted to work with. Several months later I started my new assignment and everything

seemed great. This Valentino guy wasn't so bad. I didn't get it. Why were people avoiding him?

Well, about a month into my new gig I hear Valentino speaking with another Judge, John R. Schwartz and there it was ... It finally hit me like an enforcer's baseball bat, smack dead on the noggin. DRUG COURT! CLAPPING IN COURT! No wonder nobody wanted to work with Judge Valentino. Why? What would possess this Judge to work the drug court? Was he a bleeding-heart softy? I wondered. Did he have an unlimited number of "get out of jail free" cards? I'm not a hard-nosed deputy but DRUG COURT? What was I in for? Now that you know how I came to know Justice Joseph D. Valentino, let me tell you about the man I got to know.

We started working the drug court and initially it was awkward. Every day seemed to be full of surprises. Every day we both learned that maybe there was something to this drug court. Little by little we got to know each other a little better as he would open up to me and we'd discuss the drug court and how maybe this thing could work. I couldn't believe how nice this judge was. Maybe what I thought was a punishment was not so bad after all. One day he asked me what I thought of the drug court as if he somehow already knew knowing the answer. I didn't know how to answer. He just looked at me with a smile and said he was skeptical at first too. He said he was feeling better about it, and I would too. Drug Court went on to be one of the best experiences of my career and if I know Justice Valentino like I think I do, I would say it was his too.

Joseph D. Valentino ... not a big man in stature but everyone noticed when he entered a room. Everybody loves him, and I was determined to find out why.

I watched this man closely over the months and years. I figured if I had to put my life on the line for this man, I might as well get to know him well. Case after case, I was impressed with how he handled every situation. He never treated every case the same. Each was unique. You see, I learned that these weren't "cases" to him. They were "PEOPLE." He wasn't handling cases, he was handling PEOPLE. He never lost sight of this, and he gave me a new perspective on the legal system. PEOPLE ... that was it.

He was firm in his decisions, but he was always fair. He showed compassion not just for the victims and their loved ones, but for the defendants and their loved ones as well. He always managed to do it in such a way as not to hurt or offend either side. Sure, not everyone was always happy with his decisions, but everyone understood why he made them the way he did, and they respected him. That always amazed me. How can a man send a defendant up the river for their crimes and have those same people THANK HIM? "PEOPLE" he never lost sight of the fact that it's all about "PEOPLE." Boy! I really started admiring this guy.

One day in Drug Court, like many other days, he asked an in-custody defendant, "Why are you in jail?." "Because I lied." replied the defendant. He looked the defendant in the eyes and then he said "it." Words that I had only heard my father say before. "Your word is your bond. You are only as good as your word." That's when I knew this guy was the real deal.

I enjoyed watching his face light up and watching him crack his signature smile every time a defendant reached a new milestone in his/her road to recovery. He'd clap loud and hard like he meant it, because he really did. Wasn't long before he had me clapping in court. His passion for people and his caring heart were contagious.

Don't confuse compassion and caring with being soft or being a "bleeding heart." I've witnessed this man sentence defendants to life in prison on more than one occasion. I can say that he never did it with malice or hatred. He had a job to do, and even if it hurt, he did it in a fair and honorable fashion. Every defendant knew they were facing a fair, caring, honorable man who was going to guarantee them the fairest trial possible. They also knew he would hold them accountable if convicted.

Through the years, I listened to the emotion in his voice as he spoke of defendants and victims and the suffering of their loved ones. I remember the day he spoke to a defendant during sentencing. He spoke of an extraordinary young man. A basketball player. He spoke of how such a talented young life came to a tragic end because of drugs and crime. It wasn't the story he was telling that touched my heart or even the defendant's (as he told me later in the holding cell). It was the honest compassion and real sadness in Valentino's eyes, his voice, his whole being as he pleaded with the defendant to see the error of his ways and learn from it. "People" … it's always been about "PEOPLE."

I can go on and on and write a book about this Joseph D. Valentino. It would probably be 10,000 pages, but it wouldn't be a slow read. I will say that in my 20 years of working and knowing Justice Joseph D. Valentino, he has been a friend, an advisor, a role model, a constant source of inspiration, a father figure, and someone I am proud and honored to have in my life. I said in the beginning of my writings that I wanted to get to know this Joseph D. Valentino. Well, not only did I get to know him over 20 years, I grew to love him like a father. So, I will sum up with a few descriptive words of what and who Joseph D. Valentino is to me.

HONEST, HONORABLE, KIND, GENEROUS, CARING, COMPASSIONATE, STRONG, LOVING, UNSELFISH, FRIEND."

CHAPTER VI

NEW YORK STATE SUPREME COURT

In 2001 I was elected to New York State Supreme Court, Seventh Judicial District. During my tenure as a Supreme Court Justice, I presided over trials that certainly made an impact on me. Some involved families going through divorce and child custody hearings. Others were concerning felony trials that were often challenging. Regardless of the type of case, I found that my primary goal again was to seek justice while respecting the humanity and dignity of each person.

CRIMINAL CASES:

One of the most difficult jobs for a judge is to ensure that a defendant gets a fair trial in a high-profile case. While I was assigned to Criminal Felony Trials, I presided over several of these types of cases. There are a few that left a mark on my memory for various reasons. Although I may not be able to share all the details of each case because of legal reasons, I can share some of my personal observations of the circumstances involving some of these cases.

1. Protecting the record was a concern during one particular trial. The defendant was troublesome to say the least. He had punched out his Public Defender in the jail on the weekend prior to the scheduled trial date. Due to the conflict of interest now presented, I called a seasoned, respected attorney to defend him. I explained that this may be a tough case, but the attorney agreed to represent the defendant.

   The defendant took the stand in his defense. Just before summations, the defendant stood up and yelled out in court that his lawyer told him to lie on the stand. I immediately removed the jury and instructed them when they returned that they were to disregard any of the comments made by the defendant. I told the jury that I had known this attorney for a very long time and had never seen nor heard of any such conduct by him. It was important to explain to the jury that this outburst was not evidence to be considered during their deliberations.

2. There was one case where a defendant did not want to go to trial. He kept firing his lawyers and saying that they were all racist. I asked a veteran lawyer, who also happened to be a minority, to act as his defense attorney. The attorney accepted the assignment and

THE TRIAL OF MY LIFE

was later a little chagrined when he was also called a racist by the defendant!

I realized that the defendant was trying his best to delay the trial. On the Friday before the Monday trial date, I scheduled the last pre-trial conference, in court, to make sure that we were all set. The defendant, once again, asked for a new attorney with no substantial grounds. His request was denied. As he was leaving the courtroom, he turned and yelled "You're a f***ing a**hole!!" I had the deputy bring him back into court and said, "Listen, I know that you want me to hold you in contempt. If I do, you can move to have me recused and you won't go to trial on Monday. We ARE going to trial on Monday, so I am NOT going to hold you in contempt ... see you on Monday morning, ready for trial."

On Monday morning, as soon as the defendant came into court from the jail, the attorney asked to approach the bench. He told the ADA and I that his client did not want a jury trial, that he wanted to go "bench." Somewhat surprised, I said to the attorney, "That's OK with me, but please remind your client that he will be going to trial in front of the f***ing a**hole!."

SIDEBAR

There was also a case around that time with a defendant who continually represented himself. He would sue judges on a regular basis so that they would have to recuse themselves.

This defendant didn't sue me and I was assigned all of his cases! He later ended up in federal court, threatened a witness and landed himself in federal prison. Maybe he should have sued the federal judge.

---

3. Another high-profile trial involved a double murder and a serious assault. The defendant was accused of murdering his wife and daughter and seriously injuring his other daughter.

    The first order of business was to pick a fair and impartial jury. Jury selection, conducted out of the courtroom in the jury room, lasted at least two weeks due to the high volume of publicity. Jurors were brought in, one by one, for them to reveal if they already knew anything about the case. Jurors who had preconceived notions about the case were excused from serving on this jury.

    The second order of business was to give due attention to the defenses that the defense attorneys offered throughout the trial. One of which was no intent due to amnesia. The defendant claimed that he did not remember the events that occurred after he was struck in the head with a frying pan. There are many legal issues to be discussed and determined when this defense is raised because of the nature of the case. Valerie, my Law Clerk, worked extremely hard on all legal issues.

On the first day of trial, when I sat on the bench looking out into the courtroom, I realized that the defendant's family was seated on the right-hand side, all directly behind the defendant's table. The victims' family was seated on the left side of the courtroom, all behind the ADA's table. It occurred to me that probably the last time these two families were seated in that manner was at the wedding of the defendant and his victim wife. The crime of murder is the greatest of human tragedy.

4. Before sentencing at the end of a Reckless Manslaughter trial, the father of the girl who died was allowed to address the court. He stood nervously before the bench, with a sadness in his eyes. He took a picture of his daughter out of his wallet and showed it to me because he said that I had only seen autopsy photos of her. He said that I never had the pleasure of really knowing her or seeing a photo of her alive. He said that he wanted me to see what she really looked like. At the end of his brief address, the courtroom fell silent. I could not speak right away. That was one of the hardest days for me in my time on the Supreme Court bench.

5. A triple homicide trial before me had many evidentiary issues. The murders did not take place at the same time, and arson was evident concerning the elderly couple. The girlfriend was later murdered. There was evidence presented concerning the crime of arson and also a neighbor's surveillance camera came into play.

This was the first case in front of me that used cell phone tower triangulation to trace the whereabouts of the defendant the night of the first murders.

The law is continually adapting to science and technology. However, only competent and relevant evidence can be submitted at trial and the judge must make those rulings. These are rulings that are difficult.

6. I heard a case once that allowed me to preside over a trial where two juries were seated. The defendants in this homicide case were a brother and a sister. Much of the evidence was the same, so rather than have two different trials, we had one trial with two juries … deemed the Blue Jury and the Yellow Jury. One defendant confessed, the other did not. Therefore, one jury heard the confession testimony in court while the other was in their jury room. It was a different experience taking two separate verdicts.

7. The "body parts" trial was quite interesting with chain of custody and public health issues. A man sold body parts of corpses to a company dealing in transplants. It was all legal until he, and those he employed, stopped asking permission from the family members of the deceased.

The discovery of the operation occurred when a son wanted to see his father's body before the father was cremated. Needless to say, he found his father missing some body parts when he viewed the body.

It became necessary to use DNA analysis of the victims to find out exactly how many victims there had actually been; i.e. the DNA from the mutilated bodies was compared to the DNA found on the sold body parts. Two of the seven defendants in this case were tried in my courtroom.

8. The viability of life was an issue on another interesting case. A baby died as a result of a car accident and it was necessary for the ADA to prove that the baby was born alive before they could get a conviction.

The defense counsel argued that the charge must be dismissed because the baby had no legal status as a person when her mother sustained injuries and delivered the victim prematurely at 23 weeks gestation. They also argued that the removal of life support was an intervening and superseding cause of death and, as such, the defendant could not be the cause of the victim's death.

The ADA argued that the defendant's reckless behavior caused a chain of events that resulted in a live birth and the death of that premature infant. The People argued that once the live birth occurred, the victim was a person and the charge was proper.

The medical examiner testified that the autopsy on the baby revealed a deep tissue hemorrhage in her scalp and bleeding around the brain, which, in the Medical Examiner's opinion, was the result of trauma to the head and not typical with a Cesarean section delivery. The medical examiner also testified that she examined the placenta and observed that it was torn and bleeding. Based on all her observations, the medical examiner concluded that the baby's injuries were the result of blunt force trauma and that she died as the result of complications of maternal trauma.

9. Another demanding case was where it was alleged that a juvenile offender shot a police officer in the back of the head. The officer lived, but sustained serious injuries.

    The most dramatic moment at the trial for me, was when the officer walked into the courtroom to testify. He slowly walked down the aisle with no assistance. The entire courtroom was quiet. As he approached the witness stand, the court deputy started towards him to help him to the seat. I shook my head to indicate "No ... let him alone." I felt that it was important to show the jury that he wasn't being treated any differently than the other witnesses. Due to the high profile of this case and the emotionalism involved, it was important for the jury to remain fair and impartial.

    His testimony was brief, but riveting as he slowly recounted the event. When questioning was over, he stood up and as he slowly walked out of the courtroom, once again, you could hear a pin drop. In all my years as a judge, never has a courtroom been so quiet.

As you can imagine, these types of issues were sometimes intricate and difficult. In many trials, such as this last one, it was a constant learning and decision making process for me. I now call one of the lawyers who tried difficult cases in my court as my next Character Witness. This is John Speranza's "testimony":

> "I have known Judge Valentino since he was admitted to the bar. One of my recurrent observations of him is that everything he does, is done extremely well. Every position he has held, including Supreme Court, was done extraordinarily well.

The predicate for Judge Valentino's life and all of his accomplishments was that he operated under a real sense of decency. He was fair, decent, empathetic and essentially a wonderful human being. Everything that he did reflected these fundamental values.

The Judge continually demonstrated an elevated level of competence, continually being prepared and informed about the law. He allowed attorneys latitude to try their cases within the letter of the law. The Judge was receptive and open to attorney's arguments. He was diligent when considering those arguments and meticulous in his application of the law.

Jury selection and how those jurors were treated was important to the Judge. He made prospective jurors feel welcome in the court and was engaging and thorough in his instructions. He had a great sense of humor with them and maintained a great rapport, until he read them the law they would decide about. Then he was all business, because it was vital that the jurors understood the law they would be deciding.

I had the pleasure of being in front of Judge Valentino for two fairly long and highly publicized trials. During one of the trials, I was in the middle of my summation. I saw the Judge smile and nod towards the back of the room where I observed, Chief Justice of the NYS Court of Appeals, Judith Kaye and Supervising Supreme Court Justice, Thomas VanStrydonck making their way into the courtroom. I recognized the significance of these two esteemed Justices sitting in on Judge Valentino's courtroom. I stopped my summation and introduced the jury to them both, reveling in the significance of their presence.

Judge Valentino is all about respect. He gave it to everyone regardless of what role they played in the courtroom. As the above-mentioned story indicated, he also received respect from those who have had the pleasure of knowing him. It was an honor to try cases in front of him."

CIVIL CASES

When I was in Supreme Court, I had quite a few divorce proceedings. Unfortunately, I often would see families being torn apart. Sometimes in a lengthy custody proceeding, I would stop the battle to try to encourage a settlement. I would say to the father and the mother "Look ... do you want to pay for your children's college education or do you want to pay for your lawyer's children's college education?"

Fighting and stubbornness were prevalent and sometimes the attorneys themselves were very contentious. During one trial concerning custody of the children, the two attorneys were being nasty and rude to one another. As I was not accustomed to this behavior, I called for a recess and asked the attorneys to come into chambers. Inside, they were reluctant and somewhat confused at the purpose for this recess. I asked that we all sit at my round table ... the one with the candy dish set atop. They sat with me at the table and we just small-talked while eating the candy. After a few minutes, the tension dwindled; there was friendly chatter and even some laughs. I kept

The famous Judge Valentino's Candy Dish

passing out the candy and it seemed to work! The rest of the trial was much less of a battle. This story spread through the building and thus, Judge Valentino's famous candy dish was "born"! For the rest of my years, both in the Hall of Justice and The Appellate Division, judges, lawyers, deputies and court staff would stop by daily and help themselves to a piece of candy ... oftentimes replenishing the bowl with sweet delights.

There were other notable cases:

1. I remember in one case neither party could decide who was going to get the big-screen TV. I told the father that the kids were going to get the TV for cartoons on Saturday morning and awarded the TV to the wife.

2. One case involved a husband who declared that he suffered trauma from the wife constantly yelling at him. His lawyer wanted to call in a psychologist to confirm that the husband was in fact suffering from trauma and I allowed the testimony. Turns out that the psychologist testified that the husband was not suffering from any trauma. I called the attorneys up to the bench and told the husband's attorney that his ship was sinking, and it was time to make a deal. The case was settled.

3. Another case involved two beautiful little blond girls. It was revealed that the mother had been reading the bible to them. Revelations, in fact, and anytime there was mention of evil people, the mother exchanged the father's name for those people.

4. Who would have physical custody of the children was often the biggest fight for many divorcing couples, and the question of shared custody arrangements, more times than not, got messy and complicated for the kids. In one particular case the parents lived in two towns thirty minutes apart. Instead of having the kids go back and forth to each parent's house. I strongly "suggested" that the kids stay in the original home, both parents move out, and then each parent would have to move into the house on their assigned weeks of custody. I reasoned that this arrangement would at least give the children a stable home. Reading between the lines, the parties quickly settled the matter. (I must confess that I got this idea from another judge.)

5. I would mention at this juncture, concerning the children, that the criminal cases of child abuse, child neglect and the domestic violence cases were always hard to preside over. There was a case where a daycare worker was abusing the children, and another one when a minister was visiting homes and abusing children too. There were several fathers that abused their children and I often allowed the ADA to call child abuse experts to the stand. These were incredibly difficult cases for me, because as a judge I had to have no sympathy for the victims or defendants, and make decisions based on what was fair for all.

There were a few special appointments made while I sat on the Supreme Court Bench:

1. The Law Guardian Advisory Committee: Being a law guardian is an important position and it is essential that qualified attorneys are appointed to these positions. I was grateful and happy to assist the other members of this committee.

2. New York State Jury Trial Project, which formulated suggested trial procedures, and the State-Federal Judicial Council. My appointment to these committees entailed meetings in different cities all over New York State.

3. Character and Fitness Committee for the Seventh Judicial District. This was one of my favorite positions. Members of this committee are entrusted with the admission of new attorneys in our district. It is a long application process for prospective attorneys and then an interview by our committee. It is important, because it means that the new lawyers sworn in would be of the highest integrity. This meant a lot to me. To this day, I am very disappointed when I hear about judges and lawyers who may not be acting with integrity.

4. In 2011, I was appointed the Supervising Judge of the Criminal Term in the 7th Judicial District. This meant that I was responsible to oversee the Felony Criminal Courts in 8 Counties. I truly enjoyed this administrative position as I would often visit the judges and their court staff in all the various counties.

CHAPTER VII

APPELLATE DIVISION

———⇒•◦•⇐———

I was appointed to the New York State Supreme Court, Appellate Division in October 2012 by Governor Andrew Cuomo.

Shortly after my appointment, Federal Court Judge David Larimer sent a congratulatory note to me containing pertinent advice:

"Appellate Division Judges are like the generals who watch the battle below from the hill above, safe and judgmental. When the battle is over, they swoop down onto the battlefield, into the trenches, to make sure there are no survivors. Always remember that you were a veteran trial judge, often in the trenches below, before you became an Appellate Division Judge!"

I often thought of his advice in the three plus years that I spent in the Appellate Division. I never lost the perspective of originally being a Trial Court Judge for 30 years. During case discussions with my fellow appellate judges, I found myself on the side of the trial level judges many times.

The most enjoyable and rewarding part of being in the Appellate Division was the work and discussions with the other judges, all from either Buffalo, Syracuse, Bath or Rochester. I was very impressed with their legal knowledge and always grateful for their warm friendship. Even though case preparation was often difficult, and without Valerie and Dan, my Law Assistants, would have been impossible ... the experience was memorable. As I have often stated since my retirement, being in the Appellate Division was a very fulfilling way to "go out" and end my legal career.

I recall that in my interview during the extensive screening process concerning my appointment to the Appellate Division, a screening panelist asked me:

"What do you think of the present Appellate Division?"

After a short reflection *(Is this a trick question??)*, I stated:

"Well ... when they agree with me, they are great ... but when they reverse me ... not so great."

I guess that was the Trial Court Judge talking, who down deep, will always be the Trial Court Judge.

My career as a Judge came to an end while I served in the Appellate Division. I retired in December 2015. For the 30+ years I sat as a judge, there was one person who followed me from position to position and that was my secretary, Kim DiMaggio. I sprinkled some of Kim's stories in various places in this book, but this is Kim's witness "testimony" concerning our 30+ years together while I was on the bench:

> "I was Judge Valentino's secretary for 30 years, throughout most of his judicial career. I was so very fortunate to have worked for him, but more importantly, to be able to call him my friend.
>
> Anyone who has ever worked with or for him has the utmost respect for him. To know him is to like him. And the same can be said of his wife and

their four sons. It's true that "the apple doesn't fall far from the tree," or in this case, the trees!

One of my earlier and favorite work memories is when I met Judge Valentino's four young sons for the first time. He had just recently hired me, and I was helping him set up his new office. It was during the holiday recess, and he brought his sons to work with him that day. I don't know what I expected, but it was not this! He introduced his sons to me and each one made eye contact, shook my hand and said, "It's very nice to meet you!" While they were there, I had to go to the main office to make some copies of a document and Judge Valentino's youngest son Nick (who was only eight at the time) wanted to come with me. When we reached the door that adjoined the two offices, he stepped ahead, opened and held the door for me! And when I introduced him to others in the office, again, there was a handshake and "It's very nice to meet you." I told Judge Valentino that I had never seen young children so well-behaved and polite. His reply was, "I can't take the credit for that, it's all my wife's doing." That was my first insight into the family I was going to have the pleasure and privilege of getting to know over the next 30+ years.

Judge Valentino has so many good qualities, but the ones that I believe made him such a great judge and that stand out are these:

He always sees the good in people. When I think about what he's seen throughout his legal career—his exposure to the most serious of crimes—it's hard to understand how this did not negatively affect his outlook on life and of people. But it didn't. Instead, he has always focused on the good in people.

He treats people with respect and dignity. Despite his title as "judge," he never judges people. Another of my earliest work memories is when we walked to Midtown (downtown) one day over the lunch hour. It seemed like every two minutes someone would stop him to say hello and shake his hand. I'd ask, "Who was that?", and learned that many of them had appeared before him in court, a few, I assumed, he had also ordered to be incarcerated at one time. At first I was a little nervous about running into former defendants, but I soon realized that they actually liked and respected him—because he always treated people with kindness and dignity. That was when it became very clear to me the type of person and judge I was working for.

He genuinely takes an interest in everyone he meets and truly listens to what they have to say. Whether a server in a restaurant, a sales clerk, or a coworker, if he's met someone once, he not only remembers their name, but he mostly likely knows if they're married, how many kids they have, what they like to do, and anything else they are willing to share with him. He listens to people, and he is sincerely interested in what they have to say.

He has a great sense of humor and loves to make people laugh.

From early on, when he was in the D.A.'s office, there are stories of the practical jokes played among him he and his co-workers—emptying the entire contents of someone's office, hanging a dead fish in the window of someone's office ... over the weekend! ... the list goes on.

I don't know if most people think about how difficult a job it is to be an assistant district attorney or a judge. I always wondered if the way he was outside of the courtroom was his way of coping with what he saw every day at work and the seriousness of his job. When he wasn't in the courtroom, he was usually joking, and he didn't want to hear or talk about anything sad or depressing.

On the bench, he was very serious and everything "was by the book," but off the bench he was a completely different person. It was like working for Dr. Jekyll and Mr. Hyde. That's not a complaint — working for Judge Valentino was fun, because there was always laughter when he was around. I'm not sure how many people can say the same.

He was a great boss, and I wasn't the only one who thought so. It seemed like everyone wanted my job! As many times as Judge Valentino received inquiries about my job, I was told how lucky I was to work for him. It was almost a daily ritual.

He is kind, compassionate and understanding.

Even though he was my boss, he took an interest in me personally, as he did with all of his employees. At times, he treated me like a daughter—giving me advice and direction whenever I needed it. He invited me to family parties, and he and his wife always made me feel welcome in their home. It was like having a second family. After working for him for over 15 years, I decided to go back to school to study interior design. Even though it might eventually mean that I would leave my job with him, he encouraged me to follow my dreams. He even allowed me to take a 6-month leave of absence to complete an internship.

There were so many instances of his kindness, but I will always remember and be most thankful to him for the compassion he showed me when my dog was ill. My husband and I don't have children, and he knew how important our dog was to us. At age 13, our dog was diagnosed with diabetes. Diabetes in animals is generally very treatable, but our dog was insulin resistant and needed three shots of insulin a day, each eight hours apart. That didn't exactly fit into my work day, so even though it was not the most convenient time for a judge's secretary to be out of the office, he allowed me to take my lunch hour between 2:00 and 3:00 each day so that I could go home and take care of her.

If it wasn't clear before, it should be totally clear by now why everyone wanted my job!!!

He is one of the most generous people you will ever meet.

It was not at all uncommon for him to take his staff out to lunch for birthdays, or to thank them for doing a good job, and sometimes for no reason at all. He always picked up the check. On your birthday, there was always a present and a cake with candles, and he would insist that everyone sing happy birthday. At Christmas, he would buy presents for me, his law clerk, his court clerk, his deputy and anyone else who came into the office on a regular basis! He would buy so many presents that it would usually take him at least three trips to his car (with a cart!) to retrieve them all. He loves giving.

My last story, not only highlights his generosity, but also who he is as a person.

In the months prior to his retirement, I asked him if he wanted a party. At first, he said no—he didn't want people to have to sit through a boring retirement dinner. So, I suggested a cocktail party, something less formal, and he seemed to like that idea. Then I asked him about the size and who should receive invitations. He said he didn't want anyone excluded—that everyone should be welcome to attend. (Just to put this in perspective, I've worked for the court system for 35 years and was never invited to a judge's retirement party). Knowing how well liked he is, I started to panic. I told him that it might be hard to manage and might be difficult finding a venue large enough. He said I was crazy. His sons and I started to plan the party and we continued to ask for his input. We wanted to be sure that everything was the way he would want it. Then he started getting too involved. He started asking questions about how much everything would cost. We eventually had to tell him he was no longer part of the decision process. This was after he announced that he didn't want us to charge anyone for tickets, and that he would pay for the entire party!!! Just for the record ... over 250 people showed up to honor him that night."

JUDGE-ISMS

Through the years, I have had the opportunity to share some of the "wisdom" I have gratefully acquired with young attorneys and newly elected judges. They are a captive audience because they are often there for Continuing Education credits which they need every year. So, I would get to expound on whatever topic I was asked to speak about, and I could impart my extra "words of wisdom" to an audience that was chained to their chair for the required two hours.

Also, my law clerks were always very polite as I often interrupted our legal discussions in chambers with my "judge-isms." Thinking back, I guess they were a captive audience, too.

So here are a few of my favorites after 33 years on the bench:

1. If it doesn't pass the "Shave Test," don't do it.

    In the morning, while shaving, I would often wrestle with a problem that I knew would present itself that day. I sometimes would agonize over what the decision should be. If my decision seemed wrong in any way or I had a bad feeling about it, I knew that it was the wrong decision. Valerie, my Law Clerk, once impishly asked me, "Good advice, but what if you are a woman?"

2. If there is a legal argument before you in court, and you have any doubt in your mind as to the proper decision, always take a recess. Go back to the chambers and look in the book.

    This is especially true when opposing attorneys are telling you they are positive what the law states for their particular case. If your Law Clerk is in the office, two heads are always better than one.

3. Speedy justice is not always justice.

    Charlie Crimi used to say this quite often. Attorneys often want the wheels of justice to speed up. Some-times, you, the judge, are going to need a little more time to craft a good decision or, as an attorney, more time to formulate a good legal argument.

4. As a judge, there is no need to be sarcastic or nasty when you are sentencing a defendant.

    Whether you find yourself sentencing someone to 15 days in jail or 15 years in prison, do not demean that person standing before you. Do not take away a person's dignity.

5. Always remember that the attorneys will respect the robe and the bench in court. These are symbols of justice. You must act fair and impartial at all times on the bench. If you continue to act in this manner, the

attorneys will begin to respect you as a judge. Don't find yourself contracting that self-centered and egotistical "disease" called robe-itis.

6. Listen more and talk less. No one learns anything by talking.

7. On the way to presiding in court, never pass a bathroom. You never know how long you will be on the bench!

CHAPTER VIII

TRIED BY A JURY OF MY PEERS

I won't bore you with the political history of my early attempts to run for office. Let's just say that I was extremely naive in the beginning when it came to politics. It took a while for me to become savvy. Everything turned out OK for me, however, and I am very thankful to many people who stood by me in "political" good and bad times, such as Sheila Fleischauer, Patty McCarthy, Mary Jo Provenzano, Chick Plummer, Kim DiMaggio, Karl Salzer, Bucky Cristo, Paul Leclair, Ted O'Brien, Joe Morelle and Bob Duffy, just to name a few.

I am 3 for 4 in actual elections ... two for City Court Judge and one for Supreme Court. I ran for County Court Judge once and lost, but was later appointed an Acting County Court Judge during my tenure in Drug Court.

I remember many, many of the people who helped me through the years, which is definitely the best part of running for election ... all the nice and thoughtful people that you meet along the way.

From my City Court campaigns, I remember a few humorous stories:

I used to walk the election districts during the primary going house to house, dropping off key cards and talking to whomever would listen. One day, I knocked and when an older woman came to the door, I introduced myself, "Hello! I'm Judge Valentino and I am running for City Court." She replied, "Oh, I'm so happy you stopped by. Can you come down to the basement? We have rats down there and maybe you can do something being from the City."

———⊷•⊶———

We used to cover an entire election district, dropping off key cards, in just a couple of hours. This was due to the help of car drivers and numerous school classmates of my sons. The cars would drop four of them off at the beginning of a street and then pick them up at the end of the street, after they distributed the cards. One time at the end-of-street pick up, I noticed that the stomach of one of the boys looked huge under his jacket. I asked if he had anything inside his coat. As he unzipped, a slew of key cards fell out, but they were all from our Primary opponent. I told him, "You can't take her key cards out of the doors!!" He smiled and replied, "You wanna win, don'tcha, Mister Valentino?" We distributed the cards and put them back in the doors. He probably went on to a career in politics!!!

———⊷•⊶———

Another time, a gentleman came to the door, clad only in his "tighty-whities" waving my key card previously left at his house. "Are you this guy?" he yelled twice, pointing to the card. As he was frothing at the mouth somewhat, I told him that I wasn't that guy! He just said "OK" and walked back into his apartment, door slamming behind him.

⇒•◦•⇐

The father of one of my classmates from Aquinas was involved in local Democratic politics. He offered to take me around and introduce me to his neighbors in a largely Italian neighborhood. At every house, we were invited in and at every house we were offered a glass of wine, sometimes homemade. I was told that I had to accept the glass as it would be taken as an insult if I refused. Everyone was so hospitable and supportive. After around two hours of "campaigning," I must have been tired, because my vision was a little blurry! When I walked into my house that night, after being dropped off, Janet asked, "Where have you been tonight?" "Campaigning," I replied. "Right! Must be a lot of voters in the bars nowadays." She has always been poignantly insightful.

⇒•◦•⇐

The campaign for Supreme Court was difficult. Getting into the race in July, having very little money to spend on the campaign and running as a Democrat in this heavy Republican District, were all factors that pointed to a loss in November. I gave it my best and won!! Nothing I did compared to the hard work and persistence especially of my wife, my sons and my Secretary, Kim. Our close friends were great. For instance, my friend, Mary Jo, who I've known since grammar school, and my wife's friend, Sheila, worked on all of the campaigns. On this one, they were also relentless and worked tirelessly.

Ted O'Brien is a character witness who shares what the Supreme Court Campaign and election were really like. The effort of everyone involved helped drive us to a win. In Ted's words:

A SUPREME EFFORT

"Hope springs eternal. Fresh off Al Gore's loss in the 2000 presidential race, and as a volunteer chair of the Monroe County Democratic Committee committed to proving I was worth every penny, I turned to the 2001 election year with great energy and enthusiasm. It was a "local" year. Plenty of county legislative races with no place to go but up, and an interesting Supreme Court race.

For the Supreme Court race, the consensus opinion among my political advisors in the legal community was that this year would be marked by an electorate obsessed with a radical departure from "party bosses" picking candidates; this year would be ruled by a grassroots fervor to "let the people decide." (It wasn't until many years later that I discovered that with the spring of EVERY year comes the declaration that "this year will be different" and "power to the people.") So, braced by a powerful naivety, it was with great excitement that, early in the spring of 2001, my "political/legal" team and I called a press conference to announce our "Merit Based Judicial Selection Committee" (MBJSC). And, in fact, several members of the local bar expressed some interest in running for the seat.

Over the next several weeks, and months, however, the deepening realization that a Democrat could not win in the Seventh Judicial District, particularly in a year without a presidential race at the top of the ticket, meant that every single potential candidate bowed out. What to do? A vibrant two-party system required that each of the two major parties field a candidate. Didn't a healthy judiciary require that we advance candidates of impeccable credentials from both parties?

Not giving up on the notion that we should run the very best qualified candidate, we "profiled" who that person might be. An existing Judge would be good! We scoured the terrain of sitting Democratic judges and discovered that they were almost exclusively residing in Rochester City Court. Looking at the City Court Judges, I remembered that I had appeared before Judge Joseph Valentino on behalf of a client, (a client I knew all too well), who had been ticketed for creating a wake in his sailboat in a "No wake" zone at the mouth of the Genesee River. The resulting "Adjournment in Contemplation of Dismissal" had seemed a satisfactory and wise disposition, and I reached out to others for confirmation of his judicial temperament and wisdom. What soon became apparent was that

Judge Valentino was not simply respected, but beloved. Republican lawyers, Democratic lawyers, people outside the legal community who had encountered the Judge in some capacity—everyone, without a single exception, thought that Judge Valentino would, without question, be an extraordinary Supreme Court Judge. Though, to be completely candid, the question of whether he could achieve that position as a Democrat was very far from unanimous!

Undeterred by questions of whether we could possibly achieve electoral success, and convinced that I had found the perfect candidate, a lunch meeting at the Brighton Restaurant with Judge Valentino and a few select members of the MBJSC was soon arranged. The Judge graciously accepted the invitation to lunch, but truth be told, (and Judge Valentino only confided in me after the election), the Judge had come to the Brighton Restaurant that day having decided to tell me that he was not going to make the run.

Sitting around a table for lunch, we ran potential turnout numbers for the City of Rochester, and its impact on the total Monroe county vote. We discussed expected Democratic votes totals in each of the other counties in the Seventh Judicial district, which was a scary process. We determined by how much he would have to exceed those expectations in each county to be successful overall. We suggested to the Judge that we could expect increased city turnout due to other candidate races, and that if he could narrow the gap elsewhere, he could win. This is where I learned something perhaps somewhat unique about Judge Valentino, something I knew would make him a spectacular judge. He listens! Judge Valentino, even though it was decidedly late in the political calendar to be just entering such a big race, agreed to run!

Watching his campaign unfold, I soon learned a lot more about Judge Valentino. First, he is one dedicated, hard worker! He, and his sons, were soon present all over every corner of the geographically huge Seventh Judicial District. Hot dogs, clambakes, and coffees in Hornell and Geneseo and Lyons, and more. Much more. Somehow, he seemed to cover every event in every county in every part of the District.

That is how I learned another thing about Judge Valentino. He walks into a room, says a few "hellos," and people respond to him. His warmth, good humor, ready smile and approachability made him an immediate hit with good folks everywhere. People can relate to Judge Valentino. He doesn't talk at people, or to people, he speaks *with* people. I began to realize that something special was happening in the campaign.

His reputation was sterling, but the thought that he could win was far from conventional wisdom. After the election, it seems everyone knew he was going to win, but before the election, believers were hard to find. His reputation, character, and his chances for electoral success were summed up by a well-meaning attorney I saw on the streets of downtown a week or two before the election: "Judge Valentino is such a great guy. It's a shame he can't win!"

Always charitable, after his win Judge Valentino accepted my congratulations and said, "Ted, you can use this win. Take credit for it." Believe me, Judge, I did. Thank you for having the courage to take on a very tough challenge. The party, our community, and our judiciary are all better for you having done so."

>-•-«=

As you can already see, I love to tell great stories. Here are a couple that happened during my campaign for Supreme Court:

On a Sunday, they sent me to campaign at a Democratic picnic in Penfield. I drove into the park and spotted a parking lot full of cars. Some people were playing games and others were congregated around the pavilion. My son Chris and I grabbed our key cards and began to circulate and talk to the people. Everyone was very friendly and one fellow invited me in for lunch. As I was sitting down, I noticed that one fellow had on a baseball hat with my opponent's name on it. Having such a good time, it didn't faze me. In the middle of my meal, my son came rushing over and whispered, "Dad, I've got to talk to you. We have to leave." "Not now, Christian, this is a great place to campaign. Everyone is so nice." He looked around and bent over, "This may be a great place to campaign, but it's also the Penfield Republican picnic!! The Democrats are waiting for you up the hill." Well, I politely thanked everyone for their hospitality and quietly left. I wonder if I got any votes from that day.

———⟫•◦•⟪———

One day, I was invited to speak at a fraternal organization in a small town in Livingston County. After a few minutes in the lodge, it became apparent to me that myself and maybe one other person there were Democrats. I was scheduled to give my little pitch before their steak dinner and then leave. In the middle of my political speech, I mentioned the Drug Court. All of a sudden, hands began to spring up. I received many questions, obviously from curious citizens who had heard of this "drug court," but did not know what it was exactly. Slowly, the crowd became more and more receptive and friendly. They invited me to stay for dinner (delicious steak, by the way) and many gave me well wishes as I left.

On election night, one of the chief speech writers and strategists in my campaign gave me a call. She said, "Well I have good news and bad news." "Give me the bad news first," I uttered nervously. "You lost in 7 out of 8 counties." she exclaimed excitedly. I was confused. "But you won the election!!" she yelled into the receiver. "You won heavy in Monroe County. Also, you only lost by small margins in some heavy Republican counties." "A funny thing," she said, "in Livingston County you surprisingly had quite a few votes in a normally all Republican town!" Thank you Lodge members!

———⟫•◦•⟪———

Election night was a whirlwind. It was the first time we could get up to the minute results from the Board of Elections by hitting "refresh" on the computer. My friend, Tom O'Neil was "the refresher." Everyone was nervous, but no one

Election Night 2001. Nick, Christian, Me, Joe, Janet and Tad.

more so than Janet, who wouldn't go near the computer! We received the phone call previously mentioned and when we were sure of the margin, I told the boys to put their ties on. "We are going downtown."

After speaking at Democratic Headquarters in the Hyatt, the entire campaign entourage went to a restaurant on Monroe Avenue and we had a huge party. The DJ played Beatles songs the whole night long for me—such a memorable celebration.

During the course of the campaign, I didn't have the slightest idea that there would be a celebration at the end, but there was an incident that brought a small glimmer of hope.

I met a farmer from another county, who took the time to interview me straightforwardly for a half-hour. At the end of our meeting, his hand swallowed mine in a sincere handshake. He smiled, wished me well and left. Not really knowing if he supported me or not, I still had a good feeling about this very down to earth, sincere gentleman. A couple weeks later, as Janet and I were driving south on Rte. 390, on the way to a lunch in Corning, we came around a bend, and we saw it. A very large, homemade sign, in a farmer's field adjacent to the highway, "Judge Valentino for Supreme Court," it exclaimed in bright red letters.

For the first time in the campaign I thought, "Wow! Look at that. I may have a chance."

———————

One of my favorite campaign stories comes from my secretary Kim DiMaggio. In her words …

"During Judge Valentino's campaign for Supreme Court, my husband and I, along with several of our friends, attended a pancake breakfast in Gates. We were all wearing our "Vote for Judge Valentino" t-shirts. My husband was from Gates and warned me in advance that it was a very Republican suburb. When we walked in, people just stared at us. I remember feeling uncomfortable, and I began to wonder if we should even be there at all.

On our way out, I was approached by an older woman who asked me how I knew Judge Valentino. She preceded to tell me the story of how Judge Valentino, as an assistant district attorney, had prosecuted the man who had murdered her son several years ago. She told me how difficult it had been for her to sit in the courtroom and listen to the testimony—how sometimes she wondered if there would be justice for her son. She told me how Judge Valentino would go to her after court each day and reassure her that he would get a conviction. He kept that promise and to say thank you, she gave him one of her favorite glass paperweights. As she described it to me — I smiled and told her that he still had it, and that it was prominently displayed in his chambers. It was not just this one instance — I was always proud to tell people who I worked for."

The paperweight

CHAPTER IX

I LOST MY HAIR, BUT NOT MY HUMOR

You will see later in the book, that my family thought that I rarely was in a bad mood and didn't bring my work home with me. That was sometimes difficult, because more often than not, I saw some of the worst in humanity. I tried hard not to let that taint my view on life or on people. Music was a great release for me, but so was laughing. I have always liked to have a good time and humor is important to me.

Teddy, my faithful companion since retiring, and I enjoying a laugh.

I enjoyed all of the humorous things that happened in and out of the courtroom. Some stories you may not believe are true, but each one is a valid account. They not only provided me relief and a smile or chuckle while in the DA's Office or on the bench, they also have become great for party conversation. Hope you enjoy.

DISTRICT ATTORNEY'S OFFICE

Many times, witnesses at trial were so nervous that their answers were quite interesting and humorous.

In one particular case, there were questions raised by the defense during cross examination, and discrepancies arose between the victim's testimony at the trial, and her testimony in the Grand Jury. On redirect, I got right to the point.

"We have to clear something up, Ms. Victim. Do you remember everything about that night?"

"Yes, Yes, I do." she exclaimed.

"Then I ask you to recall the specific incident where you were hit over will the head with a hammer. Where was your head at the time of the assault?"

Pause. "It was on my shoulders." came the confident reply.

———※·◦·◉———

In another trial, the defense attorney was trying to establish that the witness could not hear everything he claimed. The question was:

"OK ... you were outside the house?"

"Yes."

"Well, was the door ajar?"

After some contemplation, "No ... it was a door."

———※·◦·◉———

During another ADA's robbery trial, in my early years at the DA's Office, the witnesses all testified that the robber was wearing a blue ski cap. The defendant was arrested very soon after the robbery, right around the corner. He did not have a blue ski cap on, nor was any cap or money found at the scene. While the jury was deliberating, they were escorted to a restaurant by Sheriff's Deputies to eat supper. In those days, in almost all major felony cases, jurors could not leave the jury room until they reached a verdict. The only time that they could leave was to be escorted to supper or to be sequestered and guarded overnight. When they returned from the restaurant, they were to be escorted to the courtroom, through the 2nd floor lobby, into the courtroom doors.

As it happened, the defense attorney arrived at the Hall of Justice right around the same time and politely followed the jury at a distance. As the jury came around the corner on the floor leading to the lobby, they and the defense attorney spotted the defendant, sitting on a bench, wearing a blue ski cap. Obviously frustrated, the defense attorney leaned over to the defendant and quietly asked "Were you sitting in the same freaking trial as I was?" Needless to say, a "Guilty" verdict was delivered in about 15 minutes.

—————⋙•0•⋘—————

Around Christmas time one year, the county purchased a huge state-of-the art electronic filing cabinet for the DA's Office. The woman who was designated the operator of this machine was very controlling. No one could touch it, except her, as she said that it was very sensitive. This policy was inconvenient to all the attorneys, as our files were not readily available.

One day, another ADA and I went downtown to do some shopping during lunch. We spotted a battery powered "Christmas bird" that would chirp (loudly) while in your holiday tree. OK … you guessed it … we came back to the office and hid it deeply in the massive rotating filing cabinet. When the woman came back from lunch, she reported to the DA that she was sure that there was a bird in the filing cabinet and she can't get it out. As you can imagine, the DA just shook his head!

CITY COURT

There were a few instances regarding apparel in City Court that would make you wonder what the person was thinking!

One young man showed up in court for a loitering charge in a T-shirt that said B.U.M. on it. In another instance, a young woman, charged with drug possession, came to court wearing a shirt with a huge marijuana plant depicted in the front.

⸻◦⸻

Another time, a defendant showed up for his trial wearing a T-shirt and a bathing suit. I had to remind him that, contrary to what he may have heard, there was no swimming pool in the Hall of Justice.

⸻◦⸻

My children went to Aquinas and played sports. I would try not to miss any games. During one season, I was aware that one of the student's warm up jackets went missing. Lo and behold one day in my courtroom, not too long after, a defendant appeared for his trial wearing the AQ jacket. I knew it was the missing one because the player's name and number were readily apparent. Just before the lunch recess, I called the lawyer to the bench and told him:

"When your client leaves the courtroom, he will also leave the jacket he is wearing on the defense table. I'm sure that he will do as you say ... and there will be no problem."

When I returned to court, the jacket was on the table.

———⟫•◦•⟪———

A man in his 50s came out of lock up to be arraigned one summer morning on a Disorderly Conduct charge. He was clad only in Bermuda shorts and no shirt. His hair was quite disheveled and his belly was hanging over his pants. He kept talking and the deputies were asking him to quiet down. In the middle of the arraignment, he smiled and looked up to me and stated, "Hey judge! You've got nice teeth."

"Thank you." I said continuing the proceeding quickly.

He then looked down at the court clerk.

"And you ... you've got nice tits!" The next thing I heard were muffled sounds coming from the defendant. Somehow kleenex ended up stuffed in his mouth.

———⟫•◦•⟪———

There was an abortion protest at one of the hospitals. One of the protesters decided to glue his head with Crazy Glue to the glass door at the entrance. The police couldn't "unstick" his head so they cut a circle out of the glass door. When the defendant walked into the courtroom for arraignment in front of me, the lights were shining just over his head. At first, it looked like the glass circle that was affixed to his head was a halo. Turns out he wasn't such an angel.

One day there was a defendant in the courtroom for an animal cruelty charge. He had a dog and the defendant was accused of being involved in a dog-fighting activity. All the dogs were confiscated by Animal Control. The defendant insisted that the dog was not involved in the fights; he was a family pet, and that they were there just to watch. His attorney reiterated his innocence and said that his dog's confiscation was causing the dog and the owner undue hardship. He asked for the dog's release. I asked the name of the dog because I had a list of license IDs in front of me. The attorney turned to his client and then sheepishly turned to me.

"Killer" the attorney quietly stated.

Killer was not released that morning.

One Saturday morning, the court reporter assigned was an old friend. He was in the courtroom covering arraignments and there happened to be a prostitution raid the night before. One after another came out of the lock-up and then an exceptionally beautiful one stepped up to the bar. I arraigned her and immediately afterward, the reporter frantically raised his hand. He asked to approach the bench. He leaned over and said,

"Can we take a break?"

"Sure. Do you have to go to the bathroom?" I asked.

"No. I want to get the last one's phone number." he laughingly stated.

He was pulling my leg as he sat down smiling and resumed his reporting duties.

There were also "John Raids" (the patrons). One morning, a smiling defendant slowly walked down the aisle in court after his name was called. He turned out to be an eighty-five year old widower. When he came to court on the adjourned date with his attorney and proof of physical exam, he received an Adjournment in Contemplation of Dismissal. That meant if he didn't get arrested for patronizing within the next six months, the conviction would be sealed. In the back of my mind, I kind of wanted to tell him that if he DID get arrested again for patronizing within six months that I STILL would seal his conviction (a reverse ACD)!

This next case is a little sensitive in nature and I, in no way, want to demean a different culture at all. This did provide me a laugh or two, so I feel I should share it.

There was a Vietnamese defendant who was charged with animal cruelty because he was caught having sex with a duck. The courtroom was full of lawyers that day as everyone wanted to see what I was going to do with this defendant and the unusual circumstances. When I called his name. the lock-up door opened and as he walked out of the "bullpen" I could hear the other defendants waiting for their cases to be called. All I could hear was a loud choir:

"Quack ... quack ... quack ... quack"

Compassionately, I ordered that the defendant be evaluated by our court psychologist.

The psychologist later reported to me in chambers, with the two attorneys present, that the defendant's behavior was basically a result of trauma from when his girlfriend broke up with him. The psychologist went on to say that:

"You may not understand, judge. He is from a different culture. They have different ways there."

Incredulously, I looked at him and stated:

"If you are trying to tell me that in Vietnam, when your girlfriend breaks up with you, it is normal to have sex with a duck. YOU need a psychologist!"

———

The elderly were occasionally in my courtroom during the civil trials. An elderly woman came in, assisted by her son, claiming that she had paid $4,000 to a contractor to put siding on her house. She showed pictures that clearly and believably demonstrated that her house was not sided. The defendant, a contractor, was adamant that he had sided the house and he showed photos of a beautifully sided blue house. He claimed that they were taken that morning. I wasn't sure who to believe so I ordered a site visit of the home to see what had actually been performed. We all drove (in separate cars) to a street off East Avenue in the city. As we neared the given address, I could see a blue house. Upon arrival, the court reporter set up her machine in the driveway and I took testimony:

"Is this your house?" I asked the woman.

"Yes" she stated as she checked back over her shoulder. I guess to be certain.

"It looks brand new—like the house was recently sided." I frowned.

The old woman sighed, shook her head, and said:

"Judge, I don't know. The house didn't look like this when I left for court this morning."

Then there was also a very old man with a cane who was a landlord to a very perky tenant. He was upset that the tenant was behind in her rent and also had stolen and maxed out his Sears Credit Card. The tenant, considerably younger, defended herself and said that the landlord at first wanted the rent, but then instead all he wanted was "sex, sex, sex, all of the time."

After paying for her rent in this unusual way, she said that she took the credit card because, "Ain't this body worth anything?"

I looked over at the old gentleman to ask his side of the story and all I could see was a very big smile on his face.

Another small claims case involved a man who had been cutting across the property of a car dealership and was bitten by a dog. He asked me if he could show me the scar that was left by the dog. He motioned behind his back. I answered that he could show me, figuring that it would be somewhere from his knee down. Sure enough, he dropped his pants and underwear right in front of the court reporter's face. He had been bitten on his buttocks. The poor court reporter may never have taken a small claims case again!

━━━━◆━━━━

Ethnicity came up more than once during my time in City Court. During one particular trial, a witness for the defense, was being questioned about the appearance of a police officer not involved in the case. The Prosecutor, on cross examination, was trying to discredit her testimony. He asked what the "mystery policeman" looked like. She replied:

"He looked like a policeman."

"Well, was he a black policeman?" the ADA asked.

"No." she answered.

"Was he a white policeman?" the ADA continued.

"No." she replied, a bit testy.

The ADA looked confused:

"Well ... if he wasn't black and he wasn't white, what was he?"

She pondered somewhat:

"He looked like he was an Eye-talian."

Smiling, I looked over at the jury, but they all looked shyly down at the floor! It took less than 30 minutes for that story to circulate around the Hall of Justice.

━━━━◆━━━━

There was a defendant to be arraigned on a charge of assaulting a police officer. That is a felony assault charge in the State of NY and police always used to tack on other charges such as Obstructing Governmental Administration and/or

Disorderly Conduct. The defendant came out when his name was called. His head was bandaged up, and he was furious. I asked him to calm down as I had to read the specific charges to him in court.

"I didn't do anything, Judge. I didn't do anything."

I proceeded to read the Assault and Obstructing charges. When I got to Disorderly Conduct, he erupted:

"Disorderly conduct? Disorderly conduct? I was not disorderly. Tell me, what does it say I did?" I said: "Your attorney will explain everything they allege that you did or, in this charge, what you said."

"No" he said "I want YOU to tell me. Read what it says I said." he was yelling now.

I noticed that there were a couple attorneys in the front row waiting for their cases to be called. They were old friends of mine, and I also noticed that they were quite amused at my difficulty.

I told defendant that I would read the charging Information to him. I looked down and thought, Oh no.

"Well, it states that you called the arresting officer a 'Catholic, Dago, Bastard.'"

In a stage whisper, that everyone in the front of the court could hear, one of the attorneys stated:

"He's got the wrong judge on all three!"

—————»·•·«—————

As you read earlier, I have had experience through the years with nuns in the courtroom. Another judge, who had gone to a Catholic grammar school, also had a nun once as a witness on the stand. As she started her testimony, he interrupted her stating:

"I'm sorry for interrupting, Sister, but I always wanted to do this … 'Sit up straight, take the gum out of your mouth, and speak up so that we all can hear you!'"

———•—•———

Another nun encounter for me was also in the Arraignment Part. The Court Deputy came to me in chambers before court. He related that there was a nun outside the courtroom with her 3rd grade class. She wanted to take them into court to watch arraignments. I looked at the morning docket and saw that there was a prostitution raid the night before and there would be quite a few prostitutes arraigned in court that morning. I asked the deputy to relay that fact to the nun and tell her that she may want to go to a different court or come back with the kids on a different day. The deputy left and came back indicating that she was adamant and wants to bring them into court to observe. He said that actually she is already sitting the kids down in the front row of the courtroom. I took the bench and the parade of prostitutes began. I glanced over and saw that the nun, sitting in the row behind the children, was trying to maintain some order and quiet among the row of whispering and giggling kids. On the fifth name read, a man in drag, beautifully coiffed and made up, came strutting across the courtroom to the bar. The first row exploded with activity and the nun stood up, gathered the students, and they all quickly left the courtroom.

I wonder what the conversation was like at the students' dinner tables that evening …

———•—•———

I will leave this section with one of the Public Defender's favorite stories. That same defendant, in drag dressed beautifully, had appeared before me numerous times. One of the Public Defenders assigned to me (we will call her "Lisa") had always been tapped to be his attorney (we will call him "Ozzie"). Whenever he came out of the lock-up, he would always smile at her, and I would notice a little friendly chatter between the two.

One morning, he appeared for arraignment, and I noticed that there was a short conversation. The defendant gave Lisa the "once over" look, and the attorney did not look too happy. When court was over that day, Lisa stopped by to see me.

"What happened between you and Ozzie this morning? I asked impishly.

She shook her head.

"Well ... can you believe? He looked at my outfit and said 'Lisa, NOTHING GOES!'"

DRUG TREATMENT COURT

Hard to believe that there were funny moments in Drug Court, but there definitely were some. One of my favorites is the story of the young man who was coming back to court for his weekly appearances. His mother had suspected that he had been using drugs again, but when his urine was tested in the jury room, it continued to show up clean. She called my chambers. (In Drug Court, we were allowed to talk to the parents, children and caseworkers involved with the defendants). She said,

"I believe that my son is beating your machine."

I asked what she meant.

She replied, "He is still using. Before he comes to court, he gets our dog's urine. He puts it into the smallest Visine bottle, attaches it to his private part and squeezes the Visine bottle to make it look like he is complying with the test in your jury room." (The jury room in Drug Treatment Court was converted into a drug testing facility).

Amazing! I had this instant vision in my brain of the kid running around with a coffee can trying to get the dog's urine in the back yard! I thanked the mother for her concern and the information.

Around one week later, the defendant came to court for his normal appearance date. He was all smiles.

"Good morning! How are you doing this morning?" I started off.

"Great!" he responded.

"How long are you clean now?"

"I've been clean for three months now, Judge."

"That's very good."

I looked down at a blank piece of paper on my desk pretending to read it and I became very concerned.

"Oh, Mr. Defendant, I have some bad news for you. You see, we send all of our urine screens to the Monroe County Laboratory. We have been informed that your last screen showed that you have a rare disease only dogs have. So, you have to be quarantined for six months. Deputy, please take him away."

The deputy started to put him in handcuffs and as he motioned the defendant to the door, the defendant yelled:

"Stop! Stop! I used the dog's urine! I used the dog's urine!"

I said, "Thank you for being truthful NOW, but you know that you have to go to jail for a week for lying. Think about if you still want to be in Drug Treatment Court."

We spared his mother from being labelled an informant and, by the way, he graduated from Drug Treatment Court around a year later.

⸺⸺✦⸺⸺

One day a woman came into court for her scheduled appearance.

"We're going to give you a test for drugs in the jury room." I told her. "Is it going to be positive?"

"No, Judge, I'm clean."

I explained: "You know, if you lie to me, you go to jail for a week. The worst thing you can do is lie."

"I'm not lying, Judge. I'm clean."

She took the test and the results were positive for heroin. I told her that she now has to go to jail for a week for lying. She protested loudly and was adamant that she did not use any drugs. I told her that the machine doesn't lie. She then said that she wanted to take the test again.

"If you take it again and it shows positive for heroin again, you go to jail for two weeks. Do you understand?"

"I AM CLEAN!" "I want to take the test again."

She went back to the jury room and took another test. Sure enough ... positive for heroin again. I called her up to the bar and started to inform her.

She interrupted me: "Wait! Judge, wait. Before you say anything, I have something important to tell you. Last night I went to a Chinese restaurant and I ate Sesame Chicken."

I smiled. "I'm sorry, Ms. Defendant. It's poppy seeds so I will see you in two weeks."

(She obviously heard about seeds somewhere, but it's the opiate in the poppy seeds that may cause a positive reading, not sesame seeds!)

I would always have the defendants in custody sit in the Jury Box. The "first-timers" would see what they were getting into if they sign the contract. This would also allow those who lied, and are now in jail, to have some hope when they saw and heard the defendants who were doing well in their program.

Sometimes when a defendant was giving me a "song and dance" as to why they didn't report to their caseworker, I would say, pointing to the jury box:

"Well, we have a jury here."

Then, addressing the "jury" ...

"What do you guys think? Is he lying or not?"

Quite often I would get jeers and "thumbs down" from the very experienced jury!

In one case, there was a defendant who claimed he was caught in a crowded VW where everyone else was smoking pot, but not him. He explained that's why he tested positive. I asked the "jury of his peers" what they thought about his innocence. To no one's surprise, a unanimous verdict of "guilty." Off to jail for a week.

SUPREME COURT

My time on the NYS Supreme Court was mostly filled with the trials of major felony cases. There were also civil settlements and trials and divorce proceedings. Most cases were filled with heart-wrenching stories, so I can't say that there was a lot of humor in the court. There were a few light moments.

When a judge issues an Order of Protection, it is almost always because of an assault alleged to have been committed on a family member. In one case, a husband came into court and requested an Order of Protection regarding his wife. I asked if he was assaulted by the wife. He said "No." I continued:

"Was there a threat either verbally or with a weapon?"

Once again, "No." was the response.

I began to explain what an Order entailed and that there had to be a valid reason.

"I have a valid reason, judge. My wife is tossing some other guy's salad." he angrily spurted.

Not being familiar with that expression, but realizing that he was not talking about any culinary event; I looked at the court clerk. She looked up, blushed a bit and whispered:

"His wife is unfaithful, Judge."

I explained, once again, what an Order of Protection was and that I wouldn't sign one for tossing a salad.

Another case, not mine, but worthy of relating, involved a visiting rural county judge who was assisting the Monroe County judges. I was told that a man from a Third World country was looking to also get an Order of Protection. The judge asked why. The answer was simple, according to the man:

"My wife doesn't cook or clean the house. She sits around and watches TV all day."

The judge, probably holding back a giggle, explained that those were not reasons for an Order.

"You don't understand, judge. I paid 20 cows for that woman!" the man pleaded.

"OK." said the judge "We will put this over until next Friday so that both parties can come into court."

The court clerk asked to approach the bench. She politely explained to the visiting judge:

"Please understand, Judge, the judges don't adjourn these cases to a new date."

He smiled and stated, "YOU don't understand. I'm from a rural county. I want to see what a 20 cow woman looks like!!"

<hr />

We were in the middle of jury selection on one case. I would always ask the general question at the end of the specifics if there was any other thing that would prevent a juror from being fair and impartial. One of the prospective jurors raised his hand and asked to approach the bench. He obviously had something private to tell me. The ADA and Defense Attorney accompanied him to the bench.

"What's the problem?" I asked.

He looked around at the attorneys and then looked at the court clerk, nodding his head in her direction.

"Judge, I have to tell you that if I am picked as a juror, I cannot give it my full attention. I would be distracted by your beautiful court clerk. I won't be able to take my eyes off her for the whole trial!" he exclaimed with frustration in his voice.

Both attorneys, stifling a laugh, said that they would have no objection if the juror was excused. The juror looked relieved.

I said "Look, I really don't believe a single word you stated, but I must admit that's the most ingenious excuse I have ever heard to get out of serving as a juror!

During jury selection, a judge must always insure that there will be fair and impartial jurors. Where there is anticipated evidence that will depict violence or there may be photos showing bloody scenes, I would always ask the jurors if they could view this type of evidence and if they could remain fair and impartial. I excused anyone with a problem considering this type of evidence. During one of the murder trials, the Deputy Medical Examiner was on the stand testifying. As he was answering questions, photos were displayed on the large monitors in the courtroom. After one particularly bloody photo went up on the screen, I heard a loud "thump" come from the direction of the jury. I looked over and saw only 13 heads (12 jurors and 2 alternates were originally seated). One of the jurors passed out. Needless to say, there was a commotion. I removed the other jurors from the courtroom and the deputy sheriffs moved quickly to get aid to the fainted juror. I turned to the Deputy Medical Examiner, still on the stand and asked, "Doctor, can you help out that fellow?"

He promptly replied, "I am sorry, no. I only work on dead people."

He wasn't smiling ... I think he was serious!!!

Throughout my career, I enjoyed practical jokes. They often eased the daily stress. I was also on the receiving end of quite a few. One of my favorite practical joke stories is told by my secretary Kim DiMaggio:

"It was April Fool's Day several years ago. I had recently been shown a trick where you attach a coin to the downspout of a faucet using a small rubber band. When the water is turned on, the water shoots out sideways at the person. Judge Valentino didn't have court that afternoon, so I decided to try it on him. I rigged up the faucet while he was at lunch. After returning, he went into his chambers and closed the door and I patiently waited for my reward! It seemed like hours had gone by. Finally, I heard the door to his bathroom close. After a few minutes, I heard a yell from within the bathroom, but it wasn't Judge Valentino's voice!!

Instead of Judge Valentino being "the brunt of my joke," it was the Administrative Judge of the Seventh Judicial District. He had entered Judge Valentino's chambers from the back entrance, and during their (unscheduled) meeting, he asked to use the bathroom to wash his glasses. He was just the perfect height to get soaked in the worst possible area! If that wasn't bad enough Judge Valentino offered to accompany him back to his chambers, walking in front of him, so that no one would see the large wet spot on his pants. Judge Valentino came back to my office and "calmly" suggested that I go and apologize, which I did (several times). The good news (for me) was that I had worked with the Administrative Judge in the past and he knew I wasn't a total idiot. Did I mention that it was a beautiful silk suit?!! Did I mention how nice it was of Judge Valentino to let me keep my job?"

CHAPTER X

HOME COURT ADVANTAGE

———⇒»·◦·«⇐———

As I indicated earlier, I would have never been successful as a judge without all the love and support I received at home. I must admit that my wife, Janet, shouldered a great deal of the responsibility of raising our four boys. Quite often, because of the demands of my job, running for office and teaching, she was home alone with them. She is the backbone of our family.

We met when I was a student at St. John's University. She was ready to go back to England after working for a year as an Au Pair on Long Island. I proposed on St. Patrick's Day (like a good Italian) in my second year of Law School. In my last semester of my third year, I ran out of money, and I really was reluctant to bother my parents who had already sacrificed so much. Janet came through for me and paid for my last semester. Thinking back, that was a risk. We weren't even married yet!! We were married on August 7, 1971. She is not Catholic, but got along famously with the Monsignor who married us. Prior to our marriage, they would have "discussions" about birth control and other things pertaining to the Catholic Church.

Fast forward to around ten years after our wedding. The whole family was at a carnival in Irondequoit. Janet, stopping at a booth alone, turned and saw the Monsignor. They greeted one another, and he asked if we had any children. My wife whistled loudly and all four sons came running and stood there, surprisingly in order of age.

"So much for birth control, Monsignor." was her laughing introduction to the kids.

I must say that she has stood by me, all these years, through the good and the bad. The bottom line was that I had to learn to leave all the controversy at the Hall of Justice when I came home at night. Peace at home is what she managed to sustain through the years.

Often, when I would ask her for some advice, she would say that she didn't want to give an opinion, but I always instinctively knew what it was! One time when she gave an opinion (kinda) was in July of 2001, when I was agonizing over whether to run for New York State Supreme Court. As a Democrat, in a heavy Republican district, my chances of winning were slim. I asked her, "OK, tell me, what do you think?" True to form, she exclaimed, "I am not going to say yes or no. It's your decision ..." Pause. "But, if you say no and the morning after the election you go downstairs and open the morning paper to see that the Democratic candidate won the election, I don't want to hear about it for the rest of our lives." I guess that was what I needed, and she knew it!!!

My sons are great. Sometimes it was a challenge, but watching and guiding them in their growing years was the most fulfilling experience a father could ever ask for in life. They have made me very happy to see all the accomplishments in their lives. They have also made me very proud through the years ... in the classroom, on the soccer fields, basketball courts, boxing rings and in all their other endeavors. I am especially proud of them for their choice of wives. All four of my daughters-in-law are intelligent and beautiful (inside and out) women. They have given me nine grandchildren—an absolute joy—especially at holiday time.

It would be absolutely impossible to list all my friends who have stuck by me through all these years. I know that I haven't come close to mentioning everyone, either by name or not. I sincerely apologize to those not cited. Some have passed away, but many are still with me.

So, I guess I would take the opportunity to say, "thank you" to all for the Home Court Advantage. I would have never been sitting at this keyboard today, writing about my experiences through the years, without you.

I LOVE THE MUSIC

Home Court Advantage has to include the music. Often, in days of stress, I would go into an upstairs room, close the door, and blast away on the guitar.

Many friends were made through my love of music. I spoke earlier of my days at college playing in a band. I couldn't stay away from the music as I grew older, but fitting it in was sometimes difficult and problematic. Enter Giuseppe' Scungili.

First the music "history." We were sophomores in college and The Krax, in spite of our non-serious music attitude, was slowly becoming a popular beer blast band (two guitars, drums and lead singer). A defining moment for us was when a freshman walked into a practice one night and played a few tunes. Playing a guitar, a harmonica and singing, Jim Brucato, from Buffalo, blew us away. (He, in recent years, was elected to the Buffalo Music Hall of Fame). The decision was made that one of us had to become the bass player. Well, I was the worst guitar player of the three, so guess who got the nod? I went home to trade in my Gretsch Firebird (I wish I had it today!) for a Hofner bass guitar (which I DO have today). When I brought it home before returning to Niagara, my mother was dismayed. "This one only has four strings. The other had six!"

The reason I relay that story to you was that the Hofner was the beginning of my serious love for music and playing music in various bands. As indicated, the love of music got me through the stress quite often and gave me the "home court advantage."

The Krax: me, Jimmy Brucato, Joe Sacco, Ande Tursi and Joe Torre

When I was in the DA's Office, ADAs Karl Salzer, Bob Brennan, Larry Andolina and John Connell decided to form a singing group for one of the picnics, with me accompanying them on guitar. It was great for me to get back to the guitar again, so I tried to think of a way to play more often.

Then election to City Court came and playing in any type of band was put on the back burner. There were conflicts of interest looming if I played in a group for money, and I didn't want to do anything unethical. Soon, however, the requests came in, "Can you get a band to back The Annex Cadillacs (the 4 ADAs) for a charity event?" I realized that this idea may be what I needed. I called old musician friends, new ones, and after a few practices, a charity-only band was formed. Many of the musicians played in other bands, but were willing to play free for charities, now and then.

We needed a name. We couldn't be called Judge Valentino's band, for sure, due to ethics restrictions. Someone suggested that it be Giuseppe' "Something's" band. My friend, Russ Schaad, played with a band in Colorado called The Screamin' Seagull Revue. One of my friends from Italy said that a "Giuseppe' Scungilli" in Italy was a derogatory term for a goofy person. Introducing Giuseppe' Scungili & The Screamin' Seagull Revue!

Yes, Scungili is spelled in error. We had to fit it properly in a sign, so we made sure there were eight letters in the first and last name. Plus, a goofy person would have naturally spelled it incorrectly!

Guiseppe Scungili and The Screamin Seagull Revue: First row: Tom Homer, Al Keltz, Flora Allen, Guiseppe, Ernie Santoro, Back Row: Daryl Greenway, Chris McGlen, Sam Palermo, Dave Cuff, Tom Bruce, Chuck Noce

Well, the band has had numerous personnel changes in the last 40 years. Every musician unselfishly giving their time and talent to various charities, raising thousands of dollars through the years. We still do six or seven charity events every year, and I am very fortunate to still have the friends and the music.

One of the band members, Al Keltz, is a great friend and also a Character Witness. He is called to share his testimony about the band. Enjoy!

I AM A SEAGULL

"I am not a judge, I am not an attorney, nor was I ever in the DA's office. I also don't think I could ever be much of a criminal. No, in fact I've never been linked with many folks in the legal field or justice department.

However, I have been accused of being a guitar player, and I'm in the band.

And that band is . . . Ready? . . . Wait for it . . .

"Giuseppe Scungili and the Screamin' Seagull Revue"

Joe Valentino is a.k.a. "Giuseppe Scungili." That's how I've known him for over 15 years.

The band came to be when a bunch of guys from the DA's office decided to form an acappella do-wop group they named "The Annex Cadillacs." Appropriate since they all worked in a building addition at the DA's office called "The Annex."

Somewhere along the way, Giuseppe put together a band to back up the Cadillacs. You see, Giuseppe has a lot of experience in the music business having played music most of his life and even helping to put himself through college by playing in bands at clubs, frat parties, for dances, etc.

The band needed a name and Joe needed a stage name. This would help keep his legal career and his musical persona separate. He once told me that in Italy, a "Giuseppe Scungili" was a funny or goofy guy, so he chose that name for himself. I don't know where the "Screamin' Seagull" thing came from; it was way before my time.

Somewhere around the year 2000, the Annex Cadillacs decided to reunite for a gig and Giuseppe rounded up the Seagulls to back them up.

THE "FORK IN THE ROAD"

Their guitar player at the time couldn't make the gig and one of the singers that happened to work in the same place as I did suggested that I might be able to fill in. I have to admit that I was a little apprehensive. I mean, this guy has a band full of attorneys, investigators, DAs, etc.? What in heaven's name am I getting myself into? But it was just one gig so I said, "Where's the rehearsal? I'll give it a shot."

I've been part of it ever since.

Being in bands can be difficult, dealing with personality conflicts, inflated egos, and such. But this group was different. This band was FUN! Giuseppe and the crew must have thought I fit in, because one gig led to another and another and here we are still at it.

And 99.9% of its success is because of Giuseppe. He just has this infectious, positive attitude about things in general that I find rather rare. I think we all know people that are constantly complaining, griping and looking on the dark side of life, seeming to want to bring everyone down to that level. But not Giuseppe. It's his enthusiasm, energy, organization and desire to make music with all of us that keeps this thing going. He builds us up and he's the glue that keeps it all together. It wouldn't continue to exist without him.

Through the years, I've come to realize that this outlook must have also helped him through his judicial career. It became obvious that he's earned the respect of colleagues, friends, other judges, police, etc. regardless of political persuasion and even from many people that ended up interacting with him from the "other side" of the bench. The judge's bench sits high above the courtroom, but I've never heard anyone say that he looked down on people from up there.

Part of Joe's career was in presiding over drug court. I recall more than one time when I'd been out with him and Judge Schwartz (who started the local drug court) and witnessed folks stopping by to say, "Hello." People would sometimes say, "Remember me? I want to say, thanks. You helped me out when I needed it and now I'm back on track."

That must be very satisfying.

I don't know if Joe thinks much about what kind of legal legacy he's leaving behind. Now that he's retired, I guess it must cross his mind. However, I think there's one thing that he'd agree is the part of his legacy that he's most proud of, his family.

It's sometimes said that you can tell a lot about a guy's character by looking at his family. Joe's sons and daughters-in-law are the kind of people that any parents would be proud to call their own. Although I always kid him about how his wife Janet deserves all of the credit and how she's a "saint" for putting up with him all these years, (and that's true!) I have to admit that maybe Joe had more than just a little to do with it.

I'm proud that the Valentinos have made my wife Roxanne and me an honorary part of their family, and to be able to say that Giuseppe Scungili calls me his friend.

And if I've said anything nice about him in this, please keep it just between us. I wouldn't want him to think that it might ever happen again!

Congratulations Giuseppe Scungili!"

⇒⊷⊶⇐

One other Character Witness is a friend that I first met in college. He would come and see The Krax then, but now Tom O'Neil has become a cherished family friend over the years and certainly part of my home court advantage. In Tom's words:

"I first met Joe in the Fall of 1966 in the student Center at Niagara University where we were both students. Joe was always surrounded by people as they seemed drawn to him. He was well known to many since he was the bass player in a very popular rock group, the Krax. More than that he was a nice person. I spent many nights at the Monte Carlo and other NU socials where the Krax played.

Joe was and still is a tremendous Beatles fan. The band was famous for its ability to re-create Beatles songs, often no more than a day after they came out. Music was very important to Joe and continues to be to this day through his alter ego — Giuseppe Scungili. His appearance in those days was a lot different than it is now. Some people may find this hard to believe, but Joe rocked long hair, often worn in a ponytail. If I remember right he also had an occasional moustache. Joe is two years older than I am, so at college we were acquaintances, not close friends.

After Joe graduated in 1968, we did not see each other for many years. We re-connected in 1982, I think, when by some happenstance his youngest and my oldest started kindergarten together at the same school. It was then that our friendship began to grow to what it is today.

Joe does not put on airs. He is the same now as he always was, no matter the growing impor-tance of his jobs. He is extremely friendly and very humorous. He is quick with compliments. Whenever he sees someone he always asks how they are and then sincerely looks at them to "tell me what's going on." Many people say this but Joe actually means it and listens intently as the person does just that.

Joe would occasionally call and ask if I wanted to go on an "investigation" with him. I'm not sure if that began when he was an ADA or on the bench. What this means is that we would go together to a local establishment (often O'Loughlin's) to investigate if they were serving legal beverages. This was really just two or three friends going out for a beer on a warm summer night.

Our families often did things together. Joe and Janet and my wife and I went out for dinner, concerts, etc. Joe and I put on rock music shows/ dances to raise money for our kids' school. We often had local music celebrities play for free at these events primarily due to Joe's connections. As the older generation of Valentino's and O'Neil's passed on we realized that our holiday celebrations were becoming too small. Consequently, we decided to merge our families for Thanksgiving and Christmas. Valentino's hosted Thanksgiving and we hosted Christmas Eve—a tradition that still carries on to this day, some 20 years or so later.

I think the most impact Joe had was when he presided over the Drug Court. There he treated defendants with compassion and understanding. If you obeyed the rules of the Court, Joe was more than happy to give you a second chance and not cause the person's life to be ruined. On more than one occasion when I have been out socially with Joe, people have come up to him and thanked him for that second chance. They were proud to tell him what they had made of themselves, thanks to the way Joe treated them in court. I know those moments touched Joe.

Lastly, I know that there have been people that hold me in a higher regard simply because I am a friend of Joe's. They must figure if I am a friend of Joe's, I must be all right. I think that says it all to illustrate the character of Joseph Valentino."

MY FAMILY

I have shared with you how proud I am of my wife and my sons. My family has caused me tremendous joy and they keep me grounded in what is really important. After presenting my case in these pages, keeping to proper trial format, it is only fair that they are called as witnesses. I am sincerely humbled and grateful for their testimony.

JANET VALENTINO

"Joseph and I met in New York City where I was working and he was in his second year of law school. It didn't take long before I realized that I had met somebody very special. We dated for 18 months and then got married and moved to Rochester. He had wonderful parents that we lived with for a while and then he had to start his army service in Georgia. As the Vietnam War was slowing down, his class was sent home after his officer training class finished. So, we were ready to start our normal married life which turned out not to be too normal. As a wife, life with Joseph has been very interesting with ups and downs like everyone else, but he seemed to be able to smooth out any problems.

It was challenging for him as an only child to have four boys, five and a half years to newborn, running around at all times, but he adapted to be a great dad and always made sure to be with them as often as he could.

When he started his work as a lawyer he sometimes brought home cases to work on. I noticed that he always wanted to do what was right. Later when he was asked to run for a judgeship, his character and demeanor were what was needed for that position. I knew he would always be honest and fair just as he was at home.

I have been very lucky to have met and married such a loving, giving and caring person, having four sons, each one has made us proud to be their parents and their four wives, who we think of as the daughters we never had. (Although we do thank their parents for raising them through their teenage years.) Our nine grandchildren love their Nonno. (Nonno is the name the grandchildren call Joseph.) One of them thinks his name should be changed to Yesyes. I agree."

"Growing up, the awe I had for my dad was probably similar to the awe other kids had for their dads. My dad was my protector, and helper, and really anything I needed him to be. He was always there for me. He was my Superman. It seemed like he knew how to do everything, and he took the time to show and explain things to me. Little things like tying my shoes or shooting a basketball or helping me with homework. Dad was a fun dad who taught me mostly by example.

As people grow up and mature they learn whether their dad is really Superman. Just like the real Superman, my dad worked at the Hall of Justice. In 1999, I had the fortunate opportunity to begin working at the Hall of Justice. You can learn a lot about your dad when you work in the same building. We did not work directly together, but I got the chance to see him almost every day—often seeking out his advice on legal issues. Working at the Hall of Justice allowed me to see a different side of my dad, the work side.

As I have done all my life, I watched my dad. I studied him at work because I wanted to be like him. What has always impressed me the most about dad is the manner in which he treats and interacts with people. Dad is very social. He constantly acknowledges people as he walks by them—sometimes with a nod or a smile or a "hello." There is an openness to dad. Often that nod or smile turned into a handshake or even a hug. Dad has always displayed a genuine interest in other people's well-being.

Because Dad is this way, I noticed that other workers, all kinds of workers in the Hall of Justice, happily returned Dad's kindness. Clerks, lawyers, maintenance workers, judges, deputies, Democrats, Republicans, Conservatives, you name them—it seems like everyone is Dad's friend. It became clear to me that I was not the only one who thought my dad was super.

Then, at the end of 2015, Dad decided to retire. It was a sad day for me. My dad was no longer with me in the same building each day. However, his legacy of kindness remains. Not a day goes by without someone coming up to me to talk about my dad. They say things like, "How is your dad doing?" "I miss your dad." "Please say hello to your dad for me." "I want to tell you what your dad did for me." "I have this great story about your dad." These people do not have to say any of these things about my dad to me, but I feel like they want to tell me these things about my dad. Their inquiry is not superficial; it always seems like they are asking because of a genuine fondness for my dad. These daily interactions make me very proud of my dad. It makes me feel good that others see him as I do.

Dad has had much success as a judge. He is a great listener who often brought balance to the adversarial world of the courts. Much has been said or written about my dad over the years. Words such as integrity, fair, even-tempered and respectful are a few of them. These deserving words are being used to describe my dad as a judge. But my favorite way to describe my dad is as a person, not a judge. Dad really has figured out this world by simply being a kind, caring and honest person. He has taught me by example how to live life, and I sincerely hope that I can pass on his way of making an effort to be kind and thoughtful of others to my children.

He is truly Superman."

CHRISTIAN VALENTINO

"A work colleague of mine asks me from time-to-time: "What does it feel like to have a father that is cooler than you?" Each time he asks, I chuckle, but acknowledge it is true. My colleague is referring to the fact that my father has achieved incredible success in the legal profession in this community, is adored by everyone he meets, can capture the attention of an entire room by knowing how to tell an interesting story, and is an incredible guitar player in a very sought-after local band, amongst other traits. However, the word "cool" means different things to different people, and it is a tough character trait to succinctly define. "Cool" means, well, "cool." I feel incredibly blessed to call Joseph Valentino my father—my dad—my "cool dad." Below is how I define that term.

My father taught me that being an individual for the good of the family is "cool." I am one of four boys, all very close in age, and all with similar interests. Yet, my father was able to make every one of us feel unique—special. He taught us how to be individuals. He taught us to set goals, and that hard work and perseverance was necessary to achieve those goals. Actions speak louder than words. He also taught us that we, as a family, should celebrate each other's achievements and do whatever is necessary to help each other achieve those goals. Support each other. An individual achievement is a family achievement—the whole is only as good as the sum of its parts, right? To this day, as adults, my brothers and I still demonstrate these traits and try to instill those traits to our children. How cool is that?

My father taught me that respecting others is "cool." When I was a child, although my father was at work during the weekdays, my father was able to set the tone of the entire household. We were to treat my mother with respect at all times. We were to treat our teachers and coaches with respect at all times. We were to treat our elders with respect. No matter what a person did for his or her job, or what a person believed, that person deserved respect. My father instilled in my brothers and me the understanding that by respecting others, and others' beliefs, you too will gain respect. The basis of a great relationship with anyone is a mutual respect. The way to navigate through differences is to understand each other, which cannot be done if you do not respect each other. This is something that I strive to teach my children. How cool is that?

My father taught me that hugging and kissing your parents is "cool." This lesson caused me considerable "embarrassment" growing up. It is difficult for a young boy transitioning to manhood to be seen in public giving his father a hug and a kiss on the cheek in front of his friends or strangers. There was a point in my life that I would cringe every time that I was in a situation where I knew that I would have to hug and kiss my father in public in front of my friends. However, I did it out of respect to him (since I knew that was important to him). The strange thing is that, looking back, it does not seem to be as big of a deal as I made it out to be. I do not remember a time when any of my friends commented on it. The "embarrassment" was all in my head. Now, I am glad that this was something that was expected of me. As a grown man, I still hug and kiss my father. I hope my two kids will always hug and kiss me in public. How cool would that be?

My father taught me that being a dad is "cool." Even though my father worked hard at his career, he was always present. He was always available to listen, but never judged. He was always there to offer advice, but never told us there was only one way to do things. He was always there to punish us when punishment was appropriate, but did it with love. He was always there to watch our athletic games or other extra-curricular activities. He was always willing to do what was necessary for my brothers and me to form and maintain friendships. In short, he was always there to guide us through life. By his actions, he was always there to teach us how to be a good person and, in turn, how to be a good father when that time came. I can think of no better way to testify about my father's character than to assert that I can only hope that my children, one day, will look at me, and think about me, the way that I look at and think about my father. How "cool" will it be when my children think of me as their "cool dad"?

So, yes, it is cool that my father sat as a Judge at the Appellate Division level of the New York State Court system, and that he is loved by everyone and can charm an entire room with fun and interesting stories, and that he plays guitar in a rock-n-roll band at the age of 70, and now has a book being published about his incredible journey in life. But, that is not why he is "cool" to me."

TAD VALENTINO

"I have always had a healthy respect and a fear of disappointing my dad. Not that he ever did anything to set up that expectation, but the thought of disappointing him was something I wanted to avoid. That was sometimes tough for me, because I didn't love school. Schoolwork was not my favorite thing and sometimes if I got a less than stellar grade, my mom would run a little interference for me when dad came home. He never yelled or got angry, and now that I think about it, he never came home in a bad mood. That is incredible considering all the negativity he saw at work all day long.

I must have been in the 6th or 7th grade, and I had gotten a D in reading. Dad was working late and didn't get home before I went to bed, so I didn't have to tell him about the grade until the next day. Little did I know that the next day would begin at 5am. He came into my room and woke me up to ask me about the grade. We had a series of adventure books that I was told I was going to read and do a verbal and sometimes written book report on, until I had read them all. I was to do one per week, and I would give my dad the report at the end of the week. I said okay and turned over in my bed to go back to sleep until I needed to get ready for school. He asked what I was doing, to which I replied, "going back to bed." No, he had other ideas. He wanted me to start the first chapter of Robinson Crusoe while he was showering and shaving and then give him a summary of the chapter when he was done.

As a dad, I find myself wanting to be just like my dad. He was such a good role model for me as a parent. He rarely if ever missed an opportunity to support my three brothers and me in our sports or anything else that we did. He even left the lawn mower in the middle of the lawn and drove to Cortland to watch my brother's soccer game once. He coached us and when he did he made sure that we understood that when he was the coach it was different than when he was the dad. I have had to employ that speech as a father who coaches his own son.

I was the third son and my older brothers were often out in the driveway playing basketball with their friends. I always wanted to play too, but dad taught me to wait my turn. I could only play if they asked me to. That was frustrating, but I see the value now even though I didn't then.

At one point my dad started the Valentino United Soccer Team for us to play in. It was great that he did that, but what was really great was the respect that the other kids on the team had for my dad and his good reputation. Dad didn't care how talented each player was, as long as they were good kids. If one of the team members got a penalty card, that kid would then apologize to my dad for letting him down. That level of respect is hard to find today, and I find it something that I try to emulate today in my kids and in the teams that I coach.

I like to think that I picked up my dad's power of positivity. My dad would always have kind and genuine things to say about people. He was encouraging and supportive even when he might have been disappointed, like with my grades or the fact that it took me a little bit longer to graduate from college than most kids my age. When I was chosen to be second string of the Senior Select Team and was so disappointed because I wouldn't be starting, he told me to trust that something good would come of it. Sure enough, I scored a goal and everyone noticed. That probably wouldn't have happened if I had started. He was right, something good came out of it. I try to instill that same positive attitude in my children today.

When I think about my dad, the one thing that sticks out more than anything else is that no one had anything negative to say about him. People would stop my brothers and me all the time and ask if we were Judge Valentino's sons. None of us have ever had to hesitate in saying yes, because we knew on the other side of that question would be a story about what a great guy our dad is.

My favorite story was when I was working at Zweigle's one summer. The butcher in the back came stomping out to the front with his bloodied apron and butcher knife in his hand. He asked me if I was a Valentino, and I was a little nervous to say yes. He said that my dad was his judge and had sent him to jail, but the Judge was a good man because he (the butcher) had deserved it. This coming from a man whom he had sent to jail. Truly no one has ever had a bad thing to say about him, and that makes me incredibly proud.

Dad set the expectation to always do the right thing. To follow through with anything that I said I was going to do is important. He showed me how to be there for my family. He would take me out to dinner just the two of us to talk about things. He had a way of making me feel special. When he was on the bench, he would always take a call from any one of my brothers. He was the first one at the hospital when each of the grandchildren were born. He showed me how to be a good husband by the way he treated my mother. He can tell a good story, and has been a captivating teacher to not just me. When he would teach at RIT, I would sit in his class and his students would be engaged. No one was looking at their phones or were otherwise distracted. They paid attention, just like I did, to everything that he taught me. I am proud to be Joseph Valentino's son and strive to be just like him."

NICK VALENTINO

"I truly believe that my father has been so successful because of his absolute investment in people. He unequivocally believes that a person is more important than their title. Perhaps this is why he refused my repeated pleas to pick me up from grammar school wearing his judge's robes.

I am often asked what it was like growing up with a judge for a dad. Most people fail to recognize that prosecutor dad was more challenging than anything else. I can recall his detailed cross-examination at the kitchen table during Case# 024873, "The Case of the Milk Being Left Out." During Dad's opening argument my 8-year-old heart sank as I discovered that my only defenses were an unreliable sibling character witness and an alibi that required non-verbal testimony from the family dog. If I can recall correctly, I ended up pleading "no contest" and received a reduced sentence of only a week of dog doodie duty.

In truth, I feel unbelievably fortunate to have the best father in the world. He is man of love, fairness, and respect. The courts and this world are better because of him."

JANET, MY SONS AND DAUGHTERS-IN-LAW

Me and Janet, Tad and Michelle, Christian and Kathy, Joe and Sheila, and Jill and Nick

MY GRANDCHILDREN

Anna, Bennett, Norah, Zach, Thomas, Emmy, Ellie, Lena, Jozy

CHAPTER XI

CLOSING ARGUMENTS

———»-•-«———

"All Rise."

I stand and walk down three wooden stairs onto the carpet below. The locked door is opened for me, and I walk into the hallway behind all the Courtrooms and slowly back to my chambers. I hang up my robe, pondering the significance of this action today.

That was how my days, as a judge in the courtroom, ended after 33 years. There were good days and bad days. Days where the Court was filled with emotion, drama, tears and sorrow. There were even a few days when humor and some laughter were heard.

I sincerely hope that in all days there was justice. As I have indicated throughout this book, it was important to me to address every defendant as a fellow human being ... never taking away a person's dignity no matter how heinous the charges may be.

From the onset of the case, I never lost sight of the fact that the defendant is not guilty until proven guilty beyond a reasonable doubt. If there is a guilty plea or verdict, the defendant must be sentenced fairly and accordingly.

Sentencing was always the most difficult part of my years as a judge. When there was a murder conviction, there was the realization that not only the victim's life was lost, the lives of the victim's family were forever scarred. Not only did the defendants ruin their lives, but the lives of the defendants' families were made miserable by this terrible deed.

Through my years as an attorney and a judge there were many somber moments, but there were also many rewarding moments. Often, the most rewarding moments came in the Drug Treatment Court when a defendant had completed treatment and was so proud to tell me that he or she was almost a year sober and close to graduating from DTC.

I have been told that I brought "humanity" to the courtroom; I am humbled and gratified by that statement. But, looking back, I only brought myself to the courtroom. All my past experiences were attempts to make the courtroom a respected place—a place where people came for justice and left feeling that there was, in fact, justice in "that place." The perception of fairness in a place where you can be heard, and a judge will listen and decide based on the facts, the law and nothing else.

I tried my best to make the courtroom "that place."

CHAPTER XII

THE VERDICT

In this book, I put my life on trial and did my best to present my case. Character Witnesses were called and evidence was presented. You, the reader, are the jury.

I hope that you have a favorable verdict in this trial. It must be unanimous as required by law. If you are a "hung jury," I will have to write the book all over again!

Seriously, thank you for taking the time to "deliberate" while reading this book. I sincerely appreciate it. And ... no need to rise anymore ...

"This Court is in recess. Sine Die."

ABOUT THE AUTHOR

Joseph D. Valentino is a graduate of Aquinas Institute, Niagara University, and St. John's University School of Law. He was admitted to the bar in 1973 and began his legal career as an associate attorney with the law firm of Palmiere, Passero and Crimi in Rochester, NY.

In 1974, Justice Valentino was appointed an Assistant District Attorney for the Monroe County District Attorney's Office. During his tenure there, he was the Bureau Chief of the Career Criminal Bureau. He also served as Special Assistant District Attorney in charge of major felony crimes prosecution. From 1980 to 1982, as Bureau Chief of all Local Courts, he was the District Attorney's liaison with all sections of the Rochester Police Department.

Justice Valentino was elected to Rochester City Court bench in 1983. He was appointed Supervising Judge of the Court in 1984 and served in that capacity for eight years. He was re-elected in November of 1993 to a second 10-year term on the bench. From 1987 until 2014 Justice Valentino was an adjunct Professor at Rochester Institute of Technology, where he taught courses on the criminal justice system.

From March 1997 until December 2001, Justice Valentino presided over Rochester's Drug Treatment Court and in March 2000, he was appointed an acting Monroe County Court Judge to preside over all felony cases referred to the Rochester Drug Treatment Court. He was a board member of the New York Drug Treatment Court Association and has presented at both National and State Drug Court Conferences.

In November of 2001, Justice Valentino was elected to the New York State Supreme Court, Seventh Judicial District, to serve a fourteen-year term. In 2003, he was appointed to the New York State Jury Trial Project, the Appellate Division Fourth Department Law Guardian Advisory Committee, and the State-Federal Judicial Council. In 2009, Justice Valentino was appointed as a Member of the Character and Fitness Committee for the Seventh Judicial District. In 2011, he was appointed Supervising Judge of the Criminal Term for the Seventh Judicial District.

Governor Andrew M. Cuomo appointed Justice Valentino to the Appellate Division, Fourth Department on October 1, 2012 and he retired from that position in December 2015.

Justice Valentino is married to Janet (Jones) Valentino and is the proud father of four sons, four daughters-in-law and the grandfather of nine grandchildren.